Durkheim and Foucault

perspectives on education and punishment

DURKHEIM PRESS

editors W. S. F. Pickering and W. Watts Miller

TITLES

Emile Durkheim, *Montesquieu / Quid Secundatus Politicae Scientiae Instituendae Contulerit*

Henri Hubert, *Essay on Time*

Mark Cladis, ed., *Durkheim and Foucault: perspectives on education and punishment*

Marcel Mauss, *Prayer* (forthcoming)

Durkheim and Foucault

perspectives on education and punishment

edited by Mark S. Cladis

DURKHEIM PRESS

OXFORD

© **Durkheim Press Ltd 1999**

First published in 1999 by Durkheim Press Ltd
PO Box 889, Oxford OX2 6GP

Printed and bound by Antony Rowe Ltd
Chippenham, Wiltshire SN14 6LH

A CIP record for this book is available from
the British Library

ISBN 0-9529936-2-7

CONTENTS

FOREWORD

The chapters of this book are based on papers given at a conference on Durkheim, Foucault, Education, and Punishment, organised by the British Centre for Durkheimian Studies, and held at the Maison Française, Oxford, in March 1995.

The subject of the conference was broad and diverse. But it was felt that five of the papers were sufficiently related to each other to constitute a coherent collection and a further addition to the publications initiated by the Centre.

Thanks are due to Jean-Claude Vatin, Director of the Maison Française, for his co-operation in the organisation of the conference, to the Economic and Social Research Council for helping to finance it through a Research Seminar award, to all those who contributed to the conference by giving papers and stimulating discussion, but not least to Mark Cladis, who has been a Visiting Scholar at the Centre. He agreed to undertake the arduous work of editing this collection and to incorporate an introduction to it in his opening chapter.

References to English translations of Durkheim are preceded by the date, in square brackets, of the original text's publication, and all references to him follow the dating-enumeration system initiated by Steven Lukes in *Emile Durkheim, His Life and Work*.

Each chapter has its own bibliography, partly for ease of reference, partly because of the use of different editions both of Durkheim and of Foucault. It also seemed helpful to provide a comprehensive bibliography at the end of the book.

W. S. F. Pickering
W. Watts Miller

Chapter One

DURKHEIM AND FOUCAULT
ON EDUCATION AND PUNISHMENT

Mark S. Cladis

1 Standing at the intersection

Prisons and schools have lately become the subject of many newspaper headlines. Although rarely treated as related subjects, they often appear on the same page. This coincidence is not an accident. Both compete for the same, limited public funds; both are in the business of shaping hearts and minds; both are deemed vital for a decent society. This volume investigates the interrelation between these twin themes, punishment and education, with the help of a pair of French social theorists, Emile Durkheim (1858–1917) and Michel Foucault (1926–1984). Although Durkheim and Foucault are by no means intellectual twins, pairing them is not arbitrary. Both have greatly shaped the development of the social sciences, and, more important, their thought intersects profoundly at the crossroads of education and punishment. At this intersection we learn much about both themes and both thinkers. Indeed, at this intersection Durkheim and Foucault serve as correctives to each other, and hence we stand there to gain the most from them.

One way to describe how they enhance each other's positions is to look at their different perspectives on social constraints. Durkheim, unlike Foucault, tells us the truth about the necessity of social constraints and the benefits that flow from "constraints" — or as Durkheim might refer to them — from the social milieu in which we think, breathe, and have our being. Durkheim typically rejected the very idea of a fundamental antagonism between social constraints and the happiness of the individual. He claimed that "while society transcends us it is immanent in us" and that in fact "it is ourselves... We could not wish to be free of society without wishing to finish our existence as humans. Society... is bound up in the very fibres of our being" (Durkheim [1906b] 1974a: 55–56). Foucault, in contrast, tells us the truth about the human suffering that flows from social constraints, as "humanity proceeds from domination to domination" (Foucault 1984: 85). Mechanisms of constraints, supposedly "intended to alleviate pain, to cure, to comfort..., all tend, like the prison, to exercise a power of normalisation" (Foucault 1979: 308). This is not to say that Foucault failed to note any enabling aspects of social constraints, or that Durkheim utterly ignored their deleterious effects. It is to say that each thinker's strength is the other's weakness: where the one has greater vision, the other is rather blind. With both perspectives, we acquire a fuller vision.

Their different, and equally valid, positions on social constraints account for their different perspectives on education and punishment. In Durkheim's view, "education, far from having as its unique or principal object the individual and his interests, is above all the means by which society perpetually recreates the conditions of its very existence" (Durkheim [1922a] 1956a: 123). Socialisation, not private self-expression, is the aim of education, and socialising individuals is a moral endeavour: "We are moral beings only to the extent that we are social beings" (Durkheim [1925a] 1961a: 64). Education shapes social beings by instilling shared moral traditions, practices, and ideals. Durkheim claimed that despite all the assorted moral disputes, "there exists a certain number of principles which, implicitly or explicitly, are common to all" who participate in democratic, liberal societies. These include "the respect... for the ideas and senti-ments which are at the base of democratic morality" (Durkheim [1922a] 1956a: 81). Through moral education, youth become autonomous and develop skills in reflective and critical thought that are vital to flourishing democracies. Punishment in the schools bolsters the authority of society's moral form of life by confirming that social ideals and practices cannot be encroached without proportionate repercussions. Likewise, punishment of criminals, in Durkheim's view, serves to reinforce the authority of society's moral identity. Punishment's primary purpose, then, is not to rehabilitate criminals or even to deter those contem-plating whether to commit a crime; its fundamental aim is to strengthen shared social sentiments.

Foucault, in contrast to Durkheim, sees punishment in schools and in prisons as an oppressive instrument that works the mind, body, and soul into a conformity via social constraints. Punishment and education, in Foucault's view, are vehicles of discipline, and discipline is the means to painful "normalisation". This is not to suggest that schools and prisons are essentially the same institution, but that they emerge from and reflect the same social matrix, the same "scientifico-legal complex" exercising its power to judge (see Foucault 1979: 23). In schools and in prisons, time and space are divided by ringing bells and painted lines that weld disciplinary power, socially constructing individuals.

These contrasting views on the nature of education and pun-ishment should not obscure what Durkheim and Foucault share in common. For both, education and punishment are the means to instil and secure the authority of social norms. Although Fou-cault, unlike Durkheim, explored in minute detail the effect of prisons on prisoners, both held that the principal function of punishment, in the words of Foucault, "is to assure that disci-pline reigns over society as a whole" (Foucault 1979: 209).

Moreover, both Durkheim and Foucault held that schools and prisons, in spite of their particular location in society, reflect a common social environment in which we all dwell. Even if we are not in school or in prison, we are confronted with the same social norms and authority that impart knowledge and deliver punishment. Prisons and schools are both dedicated to maintaining a common social environment.

Here, however, we confront the chief difference between Durkheim and Foucault. For Durkheim, a shared social environment is required not only as protection against the suffering that springs from egoism and anomie, but for the maintenance of a democratic society. Foucault would object, as did the neo-Kantian, Léon Brunschvicg, to Durkheim's insistence that individual liberties are the gift of social bonds. Brunschvicg, like Foucault, held that progress should be understood as allowing "individual freedom more and more the exercise of its right of resumption against the material structure of society". To Brunschvicg, though it could have been to Foucault, Durkheim replied: "It is not a matter of resumption but of an accession made by the grace of society. These rights and liberties are not things inherent in man as such.... Society has consecrated the individual and made him pre-eminently worthy of respect. His progressive emancipation does not imply a weakening but a transformation of the social bonds" (Durkheim [1906b] 1974a: 72).

In sum, the principal difference between Durkheim and Foucault can be stated like this: What Durkheim celebrates, namely social bonds, Foucault dreads. Durkheim investigates and champions normative social constraints, whereas Foucault investigates and finds them intrinsically problematic. Hence Foucault lamented, "the judges of normality are present everywhere. We are in the society of the teacher-judge, the doctor-judge, the educator-judge, and "social worker"-judge; it is on them that the universal reign of the normative is based; and each individual, wherever he may find himself, subjects to it his body, his gestures, his behaviour, his aptitudes, his achievements" (Foucault 1979: 304).

These different conclusions are, in part, the result of different research temperaments. Both Durkheim and Foucault were practitioners of what we might want to call the hermeneutics of suspicion — the approach that assumes that people cannot adequately account for their beliefs and actions because they often are unaware of the social forces that influence them. On a scale measuring their degree of suspicion, however, Foucault rises as the more suspicious of the two. Durkheim's hermeneutics of suspicion was aimed not so much at exposing the hidden irrationality and inhumanity of social institutions, as at exposing the reductive assumptions of economists and social theorists attending solely to private economic motives. The classical economists, as well as the Kantians, assumed that individuals could be fully aware of their motives for action. But Durkheim, with Freud and others, held that such individualistic and transparent models of human action were naïve. We often do not know why we do what we do. Helpful critics, in Durkheim's view, investigate the past and present, often discovering surprising patterns and developments, to understand more adequately contemporary social circumstances. Durkheim's model or image for this suspicious investigator is the scientist. Social scientists, wary of popular opinion and popular agreement on ostensible social meanings, are not to become too involved in popular politics. Some distance needs to be maintained. Disciplined social scientists remain somewhat apart from contemporary activities so that they can better observe and understand them. Epistemological detachment is not the aim. Durkheim knew that there is no way for scientists to get entirely outside their culture. The goal, rather, is a pragmatic stepping back within the culture and its history that allows scientists to see a larger, more contoured social landscape.

Foucault, in contrast, suspects *everyone* of not knowing why they are doing what they are doing, perhaps especially the social scientists. Social scientists suffer greatly from self-deception, because their methodologies purport to produce so-called objective knowledge about society. The very idea of the research scientist gaining critical distance through detailed observation is ironically fatuous: as the researcher gazes at her subject, she fails to realise that she and her observational tools are the subject of the scrutiny of social forces that determines her scientific procedures and identity; she fails to realise that her *discipline* springs, in fact, from the same "bio-power matrix" — the same sociolinguistic framework defining knowledge and power — that exacts discipline from prisoners and school children. The social scientist in particular, then, is deceived, for she studies society unaware of the social netting that constitute the myths of her quest for objectivity and knowledge. Durkheim, of course, accepted that the social sciences were historically situated institutions; he knew that they were the product of history. Yet unlike Foucault, he had great faith in this particular historical development. The social sciences, in his view, held much promise for the development of humanity: they were progressive, and they were a sign of progress. Such faith Foucault would dismiss as naïve or worse.

Their different research temperaments are matched by different research foci. Foucault, the extreme practitioner of the hermeneutics of suspicion, explored the ways that socially constructed paradigms of power and knowledge enforce normalisation. Although all members of society are subject to normalising social forces, Foucault focused his work on those who are regarded at the edge of normality: prisoners, lunatics, and other so-called deviants. Durkheim, the more moderate practitioner of the hermeneutics of suspicion, investigated the helpful ways that socially constructed ideals and practices contribute to flourishing liberal democracies and progressive humanism. Although not all social ideals and practices are salutary, and although not all members of society benefit equally from those ideals and practices that are, Durkheim investigates what is working well in society — our best normative beliefs, ideals and practices — in order to sustain and improve our moral vision and to create a society in which all members can flourish. Again, I do not want to suggest that Foucault dismissed all social norms as oppressive, or that Durkheim systematically failed to note such oppression. My aim is not to polarise, but to highlight what I believe are ultimately helpful, complementary differences. A more sophisticated understanding of education and punishment can be achieved by approaching these institutions with the help of Durkheim and Foucault, together.

2 What can we know? What should we do? What can we hope for?

In the remainder of this introduction, I will explore three lines of comparison between Durkheim and Foucault. We will be in a better position to appreciate the following chapters, which are focused on the twin themes of education and punishment, if we pause to consider in more detail the character of the intersection of Durkheim's and Foucault's thought. I have organised this discussion around what could be called Kant's questions: What can we know? What should we do? and What can we hope for?

In Durkheim's and Foucault's view, we can know things only in and through history and sociolinguistic frameworks; in Kant's language, there can be no knowledge of things-in-themselves.

Society generates webs of beliefs, ideals, and practices, and these are internalised and establish meaning and power. Both Durkheim and Foucault engaged in "archaeological investigations", that is, in unearthing the social, historical conditions that shape our understanding of ourselves and our universe. Such investigations cannot be characterised as the history of ideas (not even Foucault's early work on discourse); a somewhat better designation is found in the concocted name of Foucault's chair at the Collège de France, "the History of Systems of Thought". Yet even that title places too much emphasis on discursive thought and too little on practices and institutions. Their investigations, whether centred on suicide or madness, dethroned the individual thinker (who, supposedly, privately constructs a world) and focused on how society constructs the individual, the subject of social assemblage. The body, for example, which most take to be under the exclusive domain of the individual, was seen by Durkheim and especially by Foucault as a trunk on which society carves, often painfully, its own image. Durkheim's work on tattoos and Foucault's on sexuality underscore the intimate relation between the social construction of knowledge, power and the subject — even the subject's body.

What, then, can we know? We can know, according to Durkheim and Foucault, much of the nature and content of the sociolinguistic universe that humans have constructed and lived in. Yet can we know anything of truth or normativity or objectivity? Here is where Durkheim and Foucault divide. Increasingly, Foucault followed Nietzsche in the way of unmasking truth, norms, and objectivity as nothing but tools of power. In this view, we are to be suspicious whenever a statement or practice is associated with truth or objectivity, and not only the statements of politicians or merchants, but of scientists and teachers. Durkheim, in contrast, although fully aware that "the world is inside of society", attempted to safeguard the impersonal character of objectivity, normativity, and truth. Collective representations — patterned ways of viewing, describing, and explaining the world — guarantee a significant amount of social agreement that furnishes coherence and constitutes what can be understood as objectivity. The constraints of history, including the linguistic medium that sustains our thinking and speaking, carry with them the weight of objectivity and the sacrosanct character of truth.

The strength of Foucault's suspicious position is that he is more likely to prompt us to question those received truths that do not, in fact, deserve that honorific title; hence, for example, Foucault's approach has done more than Durkheim's to expose the harsh social inequalities between men and women that society has deemed both normative and objective. However, the strength of Durkheim's more trustful approach is that he can account for the objectivity and normativity that our best claims do, in fact, carry; hence, for example, Durkheim is more able than Foucault to provide normative justification for the various well-informed social critiques that Foucault himself advanced. Durkheim would have successfully challenged Foucault's penchant for global doubt, arguing that some common ground of normativity and objectivity need to be left in place so that we have a place to stand as we scrutinise other portions of our social life.

This is not to suggest that Durkheim knew nothing of social protest, or that Foucault never made normative claims. We have a long record of Durkheim's protests during and well after the Dreyfus Affair. We have an equally long record of Foucault's normative claims, and even comments that, however ironic, reflect on the normative status of his work; for example, "the task of telling the truth is an endless labour", or, "I believe too much in truth not to suppose that there are different truths and different ways of speaking the truth" (Foucault 1988c: 267 and 51).

Moreover, both Durkheim and Foucault identified and promoted a particular type of critical spirit that they deemed appropriate for democratic societies. This is the spirit of free and boundless critical debate and inquiry that can engender radical social change. Radical, because the more a society can freely criticise and debate the multifarious content of its social traditions and institutions, the more it can probe, as Durkheim put it, "uncharted customs, the obscure sentiments and prejudices that evade investigation". Understanding that we move in historical webs, according to Durkheim and Foucault, is the first step toward understanding and reforming those webs. This last claim marks where Durkheim and Foucault converge. Both believed that by examining the sociohistorical structures of knowledge and power, of practices and institutions, we can gain critical leverage on them and the possibility of promising change. This is never a matter of escaping our social webs, but of making them more transparent.

The above paragraph begins to address our next question of Durkheim and Foucault, What should we do? We should champion freedom and justice by engaging in social inquiry and criticism. Both understood that these endeavours will be better served by generating thick, sociohistorical descriptions than by offering transhistorical arguments based on such abstract notions as human nature or universal reason. Durkheim and Foucault, however, do not have the same vision of the reformed society. When Durkheim deconstructed essentialism in his writings on education, arguing that it is wrongheaded for educational theorists to attempt to discover an essential human nature and then to use education as a means to elicit or instil it, he was not promoting a society in which individuals are encouraged to engage in radical self-creation. Indeed, in Durkheim's view, we suffer from self-deception when we believe that we can create a self *ex nihilo*. Durkheim maintained that discipline — the capacity for being initiated into society's beliefs, ideals, and practices — was a crucial component of moral education. Such initiation is not for the sake of blind conformity. Discipline produces "self-mastery", and self-mastery, according to Durkheim, is the first condition of genuine power and liberty. Self-mastery enables us to develop and focus our power and talents to a precise point, thereby creating something lovely and novel. Moral innovators, which Durkheim recognised are often placed in the same category as criminals, are informed by moral traditions even as they extend and criticise them. Moral reform, then, does not entail spurning all received social practices and beliefs. On the contrary, tradition and critical thought go hand in hand, in Durkheim's view, because social critics, faced with changing circumstances, draw deeply from their social inheritance as they forge new paths and criticise some old ones.

For Foucault, in contrast, all discipline and social initiation is problematic. His social criticism was often more thoroughgoing than Durkheim's, if only because the very idea of social norms and socialisation filled him with fright. When writing on occasion as the anarchist, Foucault seemed to imply that all social institutions were equally brokers of power and oppression. It was Foucault who unearthed the buried horrors of torture, and yet from his writings it often seems as if liberal, democratic countries have made no progress in eliminating this atrocious practice but have only managed to change its form. In Foucault, as in Rousseau, one seems to detect an underlying assumption that there is always something *unnatural* about society and that therefore individuals are ineluctably at war with the artificial constraints imposed by society. When Foucault wasn't doing what he did best, namely, generating detailed descriptions of social institutions that require reform, he would often wax romantic about the self radically recreating itself. This strand of Foucault's thought, however, should not be reduced to mere romanticism. Self-definition — the desire and ability to name and define oneself — can be a worthy goal, and can require much in the way of moral courage. It also can entail insouciance. Although this is only one aspect of Foucault's thought, it can be legitimately contrasted to Durkheim's rejection of the idea that the social is artificial and his insistence that only from society can individuals receive happiness and moral sustenance. Self-creation and playfulness were not part of Durkheim's vocabulary.

We have already begun to address our final question of Durkheim and Foucault, What can we hope for? Both Durkheim and Foucault hope for human happiness, but they endorse different routes to it. For Durkheim, human flourishing requires a well structured, just society that is poised between two extremes: the excessive constraints of fatalism, on the one hand, and the dearth of constraints of anomie or egoism, on the other. Happiness, in Durkheim's view, is invariably public happiness: the individual serving the public life in a satisfying manner. Ultimately, happiness springs from the social and moral fixtures of society. For Foucault, in contrast, human flourishing requires dismantling social structures that impose obdurate standards of normality. Such standards impede happiness not only for those in prisons of brick and mortar but in prisons of the mind, where we measure ourselves by societal criteria (conveyed in relentless images and voices, sometimes loud, sometimes faint) and punish ourselves for failing to meet them. Neither Durkheim nor Foucault expressed much optimism about the chances of achieving a happy society. Still, Foucault was the least sanguine. This is perhaps because of his deep suspicion of all things social. If power clings to every social relation, and if power is intrinsically injurious, then social creatures like humans are destined to be vanquished and unhappy.

3 About this volume: mapping the contents

My hope is that this introduction can help us track where Durkheim and Foucault come together and where they separate. Their different paths should not dismay us. This volume is not dedicated to reconciling them. On the contrary, we are more likely to progress in our understanding of education and punishment when they are seen from Durkheim's and Foucault's *different* perspectives. Some common ground between them, however, is necessary if their differences are to be genuinely complementary. I have sketched similarities and differences, then, because I believe both are needful to meet the goals of this volume — an inquiry into the relation between punishment and education from the perspectives of Durkheim and Foucault.

Although I do not want to provide a summary of the following chapters, I would like to offer a concise map to help the reader navigate this volume. Chapter Two, by David Garland, develops a Durkheimian account of punishment. He describes punishment in modern society as a ritual of moral communion in which society expresses and reaffirms its values and solidarity. Garland argues, among other things, that Durkheim's work does not suggest, pace many Durkheimians, that "toughening up" punishments is a practical way to restore social authority. On the contrary, Durkheim argued that punishment by itself, no matter how harsh, cannot generate moral order or authority. In Chapter Three, William Pickering argues that Durkheim's approach to punishment in schools is rooted in his humanism. The principal goal of moral education is to instil in the child a humanistic morality, and thus the purpose and form of school punishment should not be inconsistent with a humanism centred on the dignity of the individual. Reflected in Pickering's contribution is a tension found in Durkheim's thought on the role of school punishment, namely, the tension between punishment as a means to morally educate the offender and punishment as a means to re-store, in the words of Pickering, "the sacred moral system and negate the profanation created by an immoral act". Pickering concludes by questioning whether punishment can achieve these ends in light of the waning of the sacred in contemporary soci-ety.

Chapters Two and Three, then, raise specific issues about education and punishment, and then address those issues princi-pally by examining the work of Durkheim. Chapters Four and Five continue the investigation of the same issues raised in the previous chapters, but they explore the issues by placing Durk-heim and Foucault in conversation with one another. Werner Gephart, in Chapter Four, examines the nature and role of nor-mativity in the work of Durkheim and Foucault. Both Durkheim and Foucault investigate the relation between normativity, social constraints, and punishment. Yet unlike Foucault, Gephart claims, Durkheim failed to probe how power is intrinsic to, and thereby vitiates, normative, social constraints. Where Durkheim saw a moral division of labour, that is, an intricate and harmoni-ous system of interrelated normative spheres, Foucault saw a relentless mechanism of oppressive, interlinked disciplines sup-ported by arbitrary power relations. This volume culminates with Chapter Five, which, appropriately, provides a most thor-oughgoing comparison of Durkheim and Foucault. William Ramp begins by noting methodological affinities between Durk-heim and Foucault and such shared interests as in the rise of the "individual" and the religious roots of secular phenomena. After establishing his comparative scaffolding, Ramp investigates education and punishment by moving in a graceful dialectic between Durkheimian and Foucaultian frameworks. We exam-ine, for example, how both identified self-regulation — mastery of the soul — as a central aspect of modern education, and how both charted the evolution of modern sovereignty and its relation to criminal punishment. Ramp concludes with further suggestions about how to cultivate a rich dialogue between Durkheim and Foucault.

That goal — placing Durkheim and Foucault in conversation about punishment and education — is the end of this book. Moreover, we hope that such a dialogue might, even if in a small way, contribute to beneficial social reform. Most of us are educators, and some of us participate in prison programs. Our interest, then, is not only academic, but also practical. That may be to put it poorly, however, implying a rigid dualism between scholarly work and moral activity, between theory and praxis. Both Durkheim and Foucault saw an intricate connection between social inquiry and social reform. Reflecting on the ineluctably historical nature of our institutions and practices, Foucault noted that "since these things have been made, they can be unmade, as long as we know how it was that they were made" (Foucault 1983: 206). Durkheim could have said the same. It has frequently been claimed that Durkheim was preoccupied with the problem of social order; perhaps, but "the problem" was not simply the preservation of order, but its evaluation and reformation. Durkheim once rhetorically asked of the ahistoricist, "How can the individual pretend to reconstruct, through his own private reflection, what is not a work of individual thought? He is not confronted with a *tabula rasa* on which he can write what he wants, but with existing realities which he cannot create, or destroy, or transform, at will. He can act on them only to the extent that he has learned to understand them, to know their nature and the conditions on which they depend" (Durkheim [1922a] 1956a: 66). Both Durkheim and Foucault, then, agree that by recognising and investigating the social contingencies of our institutions and practices we are more likely to discover and pursue novel approaches to public problems that would otherwise remain intractable. Both insist that we cannot change that which

Mark Cladis

we do not understand, and hence they challenge us to understand our social dwelling more deeply.[1]

NOTE

1. I wish to express my gratitude to Sheku Sheikholeslami for her keen eye, expert editorial assistance, and valuable suggestions; to Bill Pickering and fellow members of the British Centre for Durkheimian Studies for their moral encouragement and intellectual hospitality; and to the prisoners of the Pre-Release Center at Green Haven maximum security prison for opening my eyes, tutoring my heart, and fortifying my will.

REFERENCES

References to Durkheim follow the system initiated by Lukes: see Foreword

Durkheim, E. [1906b] 1974a. "The Determination of Moral Facts", with replies to objections, in Durkheim, *Sociology and Philosophy*. New York: Free Press.
Durkheim, E. [1922a] 1956a. *Education and Sociology*. Glencoe: Free Press.
Durkheim, E. [1925a] 1961a. *Moral Education*. New York: Free Press.
Foucault, M. 1979. *Discipline and Punish*. New York: Vintage.
Foucault, M. 1983. "Structuralism and Post-Structuralism: An interview with Michel Foucault", G. Raulet, *Telos 55*.
Foucault, M. 1984. "Nietzsche, Genealogy, and History", in Paul Rabinow, ed., *The Foucault Reader*. New York: Pantheon.
Foucault, M. 1988c. *Politics, Philosophy, Culture: Interviews and Other Writings, 1977–1984*. New York: Routledge.

Chapter Two

DURKHEIM'S SOCIOLOGY OF PUNISHMENT AND PUNISHMENT TODAY

David Garland

1 The place of punishment in Durkheim's sociology

Durkheim focuses upon punishment because, for him, it is a tangible example of the *conscience collective* at work — expressing and regenerating society's values, reinforcing the moral bonds without which social cohesion cannot exist. Punishment is one of society's solidarity-producing mechanisms, and as such a central topic for sociological research.

As a topic for Durkheimian inquiry, it is particularly apposite because it reveals how, even in modern society, rituals of moral communion still take place, providing occasions for mutual agreement and moral solidarity in a world which sometimes seems to lack universal categories.

Moreover, the social and moral dimensions of punishment are characteristically *modern* insofar as they are, for the most part, latent rather than manifest, hidden beneath the mundane instrumental business of controlling crime. For Durkheim, much of modern social morality has this unspoken, latent, taken-for-granted quality. The moral bonds which tie individuals to each other and to society are embedded within acts such as contracts and exchanges which appear, on their surface, to be purely matters of rational self-interest. By showing that punishment is a process which has a high moral seriousness and a functional importance for social life, Durkheim seeks to remind us of the moral content of instrumental action, and to make us more self-conscious of it. (Durkheim regarded this as especially important at the turn of the 20th century when the new science of criminology and the movement for a rational, rehabilitative penality were beginning to challenge the moral role of punishment.)

What is it that makes the punishment of offenders an especially moral matter of importance to social solidarity? Isn't it a rather specialised, narrow undertaking, important only to those immediately involved in the business of crime control?

Punishment in The Division of Labour

Durkheim's claim is that crimes are acts which violate the *conscience collective* ("the totality of beliefs and sentiments common to the average citizens of the same society"). Because offences violate fundamental values which are deeply held, they provoke a widespread sense of outrage, anger, indignation, and a passionate desire for vengeance. (Compare this with Adam Smith's description of the sentiment of resentment, felt by the impartial observer, which demands that something be done — Smith 1976).

This remains true even in modern societies, where states control the power to punish and where vengeful motives are disavowed. To think of punishment as a calculated instrument for the rational control of conduct — which is how the modern criminal justice system represents itself — is to miss its essential character and to mistake superficial form for true content. Passion lies at the heart of punishment. It is the outcome of a collective emotional reaction which flares up at the violation of deeply felt social sentiments. So, although the modern state monopolises penal violence, and controls the administration of penalties, a much wider population feels itself to be involved.

This wider public supplies the context of social support and valorisation within which state punishment takes place.

Penality, then, is to be viewed as a three way conversation. The direct relationship is between criminal justice professionals and the offenders they punish, but the more important communication is an oblique one, involving a crucial third element: the onlookers, whose outraged sentiments provide backing and motivation for the punitive response. On this account, punishment is an expressive institution — a realm for the expression of social values and the release of psychic energies. Strictly speaking, it has no objective or intended goal, it is not a means to an end; punishment simply happens in the nature of things. It is a collective reaction sparked off by the violation of powerful sentiments — like the sparks that fly when someone disturbs an electric current. But, because these reactions are voiced collectively and are organised in ritual form, they reinforce each other. The punishment of crime thus gives rise to an important social consequence, namely, the ritualised promotion of social solidarity. This is what I call Durkheim's paradox of higher utility (Garland 1990): a practice which is emotionally driven and non-utilitarian in its ostensible character, yet is actually useful from the point of view of the group as a whole.

The social reality of the moral order is demonstrated by this collective, punitive response, and is thus strengthened by it. Society's moral order — and hence its social solidarity — rest upon social conventions and their ability to command assent. When crimes occur, society's norms are violated and thus weakened. The ritual enactment of a passionate collective response demonstrates the force that lies behind the norms and reaffirms them in the consciousness of individual citizens. Crime and punishment set in motion a kind of moral circuitry. They are occasions for the ritualised expression of collective emotion and belief — one more machine for the production of social solidarity.

David Garland

Punishment in "Two Laws of Penal Evolution"

In his essay, "Two Laws of Penal Evolution", first published in 1901, Durkheim refines his thesis. He argues that although the psychological dynamics and social functions of punishment are almost universal, the forms which punishments take have been subject to historical change. In particular, (i) the intensity (or severity) of punishment has tended to become less as societies become more advanced, and (ii) deprivations of liberty, and of liberty alone, varying in time according to the seriousness of the crime, tend to become more and more the normal means of social control.

Why is this? It is because the move from pre-modern simple societies to modern differentiated societies is accompanied by a transformation in the *conscience collective*. The *conscience* ceases to be "common" and becomes a patchwork of differentiated moral domains. Overall it becomes less intense, less strict, less religious, more flexible. Solidarity in modern societies springs not from the stern imposition of shared beliefs but mainly from the experience of interdependence in a developed division of labour. The common sentiments which emerge in modern liberal society are not strict codes of shared morality but what one might term "moral ground rules" — framework values such as freedom, humanism, individuality, reason, and security — which form the bedrock of agreement upon which the diversity and pluralism of modern society can be built.

Modern punishments are shaped by these values. They are more measured and more tolerant than were those of past times, and they recognise the humanity and individuality of the offender as well as the victim. The prison is, for Durkheim, the typical modern punishment because it is relatively lenient, and is adapted to a liberal, individualistic social setting.

This thesis extends the account of legal and penal change set out in *The Division of Labour*, which argued that repressive law gives way to restitutive law as societies develop an extended division of labour and a predominantly organic solidarity. It also adds the important (though theoretically undeveloped) qualification that the emergence of absolutist political regimes is an independent variable which tends to return to harsher punishments.

Punishment in Moral Education

Durkheim's most detailed, and most subtle, account of punishment is in the collection of lectures published as *Moral Education*. He views the classroom as a setting in which young individuals are socialised into the secular, rational morality of modern society. His discussion of discipline and punishment provides a concrete illustration of his wider theory.

One key theme of the lectures is that modern, secular moralities, which are open to rational discussion and do not depend on the mysticism and blind faith characteristic of traditional religion, are still, nevertheless, perceived to be in some way "sacred" or "transcendental". This is why the religiously-toned punitive reaction still persists in modern, secular societies.

He emphasises here that punishment cannot, by itself, create moral authority. Punishment implies that authority is already in place and has been breached. The creation of the authority and sense of the sacred that attach to the *conscience collective* is a work of moral training, inspiration, and example which takes place in the family, in the school, in the workplace, in communities, in politics, and elsewhere in society. Punishment can only protect and regenerate what is already well constituted by other means — it is an ancillary to moral education, not its central part.

But if punishment is not the centre or source of social morality it is nevertheless an essential and necessary component of any moral order. It ensures that, once established, the moral order will not be destroyed by individual violations which rob others of their confidence in authority. Punishment is a means of limiting the *demoralising* effects of deviance and disobedience.

Punishment's role is to demonstrate the reality and actual force of moral commands. Social norms are like credit relations — they depend upon trust and upon being underwritten by a powerful agency. Breach of trust, or doubts about the strength of the guarantor, can quickly lead to a collapse of the credit system. Consequently, individual offenders must be punished, not because of the immediate harm that they do, but because of the ramifications such violations might have at the level of the moral order itself. There is thus a kind of "system requirement" for punishment which becomes quite apparent in the classroom where the moral order is fragile and closely dependent upon the teacher's actions. (Whether there is the same system requirement for punishment in the wider society — especially in modern stable societies — is an important question. See, for example, Dahrendorf's *Law and Order*, 1985).

Punishment's effects are aimed not primarily at the offender, but instead at the onlooking public. Punishment's real function is not that of crime control, in terms of which it is rather ineffective, but rather that of moral affirmation.

In essence, punishment is a means of conveying a moral message (Durkheim refers to it as a "notation", a "language"), and of indicating the collective force which lies behind it. This analysis has important consequences for the way we should think about concrete sanctions and their character. For instance, it focuses attention upon the effectiveness of penality's communicative process, and upon the nature of the "message" conveyed by penal sanctioning. Durkheim suggests, for example, that capital and corporal methods tend, in liberal society, to undercut their intended messages, and that punishments should "seem worthy of respect to the person on whom it is inflicted" ([1925a] 1961a: 197).

2   Durkheim's history of punishment

There are well known problems in respect of Durkheim's historical theses about penal development. For example, he overstates the role of repressive law in early societies, and understates its role in advanced ones (see Schwartz and Miller 1964; Spitzer 1975). Linked to this is his misunderstanding of the normative frameworks to be found in primitive societies. As Malinowski (1926) and Mauss (1967) showed, these were often based upon flexible reciprocities and co-operation rather than harsh religious conformity. Similarly, his historical periodisation is crude. His two-class typology of primitive and advanced societies has the effect of grouping together quite disparate societies, with no conception of intermediate stages. And legal frameworks that he separates out as historically distinct evolutionary stages (for example, his contrast between "community law" and "state law") have been shown to have operated simultaneously and in ongoing competition with one another (Gatrell et al. 1980). Far from being a matter of the old being replaced with the new, this competition involved a fundamental struggle over ways of organising social and legal life.

One response to these criticisms is to assert that they don't matter. Durkheim's "history" isn't a history at all. It is instead an attempt to substantiate a functional theory by the use of historical illustration, not an attempt to detail the concrete processes of penal change. His analysis is functional, not historical — synchronic, not diachronic. What he presents is a discussion of two, historically successive social types — the mechanical and the organic — each being discussed as a unified, functioning entity, entire unto itself, with its own specific forms of solidarity and punishment. His failure to chart this history accurately does not, by itself, disturb his primary claim, which is to have provided a functional account linking punishment to social solidarity.

None the less, the historical critique — and Durkheim's imperviousness to it — show the extent to which Durkheimian theory lacks a genuine historical consciousness and an adequate grasp of the range and character of social conflict. The historical arguments reveal the extent to which the "moral order" or legal system of any society — as well as its system of punishments — are, in fact, the outcome of historical struggles and a continuing process of negotiation and contestation. They are not "given" facts or functional necessities which "emerge" automatically (see Garland 1990).

The conscience collective

The concept of the *conscience collective* has, in Durkheim's work, the status of a given social fact, a foundational entity upon which social life in large part depends. We learn nothing about its history or conditions of emergence — it is simply assumed to be a necessary component of any established, functioning society. But despite Durkheim's confidence, the positing of a *conscience collective* is one of the most problematic and contentious aspects of his social thought. We need to ask, in what sense, if any, is it valid to talk of a *conscience collective*, especially in contemporary societies?

The existence of a level of orderliness and law-abiding conduct in society does not necessarily imply that underlying that conduct is a mass commitment to shared moral norms. Much law-abiding behaviour is "amoral" or utilitarian in nature, based upon the avoidance of sanctions rather than a commitment to the morality which these sanctions enforce. This is especially so in situations of settled domination, where law embodies the interests and aspirations of some groups but not others. For Durkheim, mere instrumental obedience and sectarian laws are signs of demoralisation and transition. A state which does not represent the collective sentiments of the whole society is pathological and cannot last long. But contemporary evidence would suggest the opposite: long-term group conflict (based upon differences of class, race, sex, regional identity, ideology, etc.) is an inherent property of most modern societies, which are, nevertheless able to function and persist through time.

Of course, Durkheim is not suggesting that societies exhibit a total consensus or an absence of conflict: one of the defining features of his conception of modern society is the fact of social differentiation and the continuing need for the adjustment of interests and the resolution of conflicts. Instead, his contention is that underneath the surface of clashing interests and social diversity, there is in operation a moral framework which holds competing interests together and provides a basis for their co-existence. The continuing importance of criminal law and penal sanctions is that they embody these underlying values and demonstrate their force.

The problem is that Durkheim simply posits this deep structure of shared sentiments as an emergent property of social organisation. He assumes, without demonstration, that any recurring form of social life brings with it a moral framework which binds individuals to its conventions and institutions. (This is why he believes that the division of labour, having set up relations of interaction and interdependency, will automatically produce organic solidarity). But in fact interdependency is no guarantor of moral solidarity, as civil wars and disputes between trading partners makes quite plain.

The problem of social order, for Durkheim, is primarily one of socialising each new generation of individuals into a way of life and the morality and cognitive categories which support it. (A secondary problem is to ensure that the moral order is well adapted to the extant forms of social organisation.) Socialising individuals into society is thus the key problem area for Durkheim, and his sociology concentrates upon the problems which arise from a failure of individual socialisation — problems such as crime, suicide, anomie, and the collapse of social authority.

But in focusing upon this interface between society and the individual, Durkheim neglects the other major axis of social life and social conflict — namely, the relationship between competing social groups (see Wrong 1994, though Durkheim does address this, to some extent, in *Professional Ethics and Civic Morals*). Creating "society", social order, and a "*conscience collective*" is not just a process of socialising wayward individuals. It is also, and crucially, a matter of subduing competing social movements and social groups who seek to create a different society and to establish an alternative moral and legal order.

Where settled moral orders exist, they do so by virtue of successful struggles against competing social visions: and where individuals are "socialised" they are inducted not into "society" as such, but into a specific form of social relations which have come to dominate alternative forms. In view of the historical struggles which lie behind the ascent to dominance of any particular social order, and in view of the ideological work that has to be done to maintain its ascendancy, we should probably cease to talk about a conscience collective and "society-as-a-whole" and talk instead of the "dominant moral order" — and the particular social forces which promote and reproduce it.

Durkheim is surely right to argue that the sentiments of "the average conscience" normally find some expression in society's criminal laws and that these sentiments supply a popular force which supports and legitimates authority. But what he fails to see is the extent to which these deeply held sentiments are the object and outcome of a historical process of political and cultural struggle. Laws and punishments do not simply "express" such sentiments — they also seek to transform and reshape them in accordance with a particular vision of society. Popular sentiments act as a political conditioning factor upon legislation and legal decisions rather than a direct determinant of them. Consequently the "fit" between punishments and collective sentiments will always be loose and imperfect — some sanctions may be an "index" of broad social sentiment, while others may fly in the face of it.

The sacred

Durkheim's notion of the "sacred" character of social norms might also be reworked in a similar direction. Durkheim argues that the "transcendental" power of social norms derives from their "social character" — the individual recognises them as the product of the superior and awesome force which is "society". But it seems more plausible to suggest that the sacredness or charisma in question attaches to "power" rather than to "society". Work by Weber (1978), Shils (1982), and Geertz (1983) discusses the way in which "sacredness" is a quality produced — and recognised — in the ritual manifestations of power, and that sacred categories owe more to the chosen idiom and symbolics of power than to the objective needs of society.

In this sense penal rituals — trials and punishments and the ceremonies that they involve — should be seen as displays of power as well as expressions of public feeling (cf. Hunt 1988; Bartlett 1986). No doubt they express collective sentiments, but they also serve as means to organise and order these sentiments, and to impress upon onlookers the power that lies behind the law. The contrast between Foucault's account of "the meaning of the scaffold" (Foucault 1977a: ch.1) and Durkheim's account (in "Two Laws of Penal Evolution") brings out the point very clearly.

3   The social necessity of punishment

One major implication of Durkheim's theory is the principle of the social necessity of punishment. Because punishment is not just about crime control but also serves to uphold the moral edifice of society, it is viewed as essential that violations attract punishments. Thus even where the costs of punishing an offence appear greater than the direct harms caused by it, there is always another consideration weighing in the balance which indicates that punishment is required. This, together with the claim that punishment is usually ineffective in respect of the individual offender, produces what I describe as the "tragic" character of punishment (see Garland 1990).

This, to use Philip Selznick's terms, is the difference between "management" and "governance" (Selznick 1993). Management suggests rational, efficiency-minded goal-driven organisation: a realm of administrative rather than political decisions. Ends are taken as given, and every act is justified by the contribution it makes to these ends. Governance, in contrast, cannot limit itself to the single-minded pursuit of expediency or narrowly defined goals. It implies a broader responsibility for the overall maintenance of a social system, the requirements of which are more complex and more political. For Durkheim, the punishment of offenders is always seen as a matter of governance — controlling crime and maintaining the overarching order — and a failure to punish is liable to produce demoralising consequences for the society as a whole. But, in fact, only a tiny percentage of all offences are actually processed to the point of punishment in contemporary society (the official estimate is about 3–5%) and so more than 95% of offences go unpunished. And of those which are punished, the vast majority result in cautions or fines — sanctions which do not convey any very powerful symbols of passionate reaction. Moreover, recent developments in criminal justice have displayed an explicitly managerial, ends–means approach to crime control, choosing to cost penal measures in the same way as any other resources, and to refrain from punishing where it seems inexpedient.

We should also note a paradoxical element which is sometimes missed when we talk of the social necessity of punishment. Critics of contemporary legal sanctions, such as Ralf Dahrendorf, imply that a "toughening up" of punishments is required if social and moral authority is to be restored, and rely upon Durkheim's work as support for this. But Durkheim insists that punishment cannot by itself produce authority, however harshly it is used: it can only reinforce a moral order which is already, authoritatively, there. The interaction between authority and punishment is a complex one. Punishment is used most frequently where authority is weakest, but in such situations, it has least effect. Conversely, the more authoritative, stable, and legitimate is the political order, the less need there is for force-displaying uses of punishment. (This, by the way, is an observation also made by Friedrich Nietzsche in *The Genealogy of Morals*, one of the few points at which these two very different thinkers are in agreement.)

The lesson of Durkheim's theory is that high levels of criminal conduct will be accompanied by high levels of increasingly ineffective punishment — the latter being a symptom of a basic moral corrosion rather than a cure for it. The solution to such problems lies in the re-activation of the mainstream processes of social integration and control, not in the expansion of repressive measures.

David Garland

The rituals of punishment

Durkheim thinks of penal rituals as a means of representing and reinforcing a morality that already exists, but a more adequate understanding would emphasise the creative effects of these rituals. Rituals do not just "express" emotions — they arouse them and organise their content. They provide a kind of didactic theatre through which the onlooker is taught what to feel, how to react, and which sentiments are called for in that situation. So state control of the penal process allows the authorities to shape public feeling as well as to respond to it. (Although one should add that the mass media now play a crucial intermediary role in this communication process.)

These ritual occasions form the focus for the diffuse concerns, anxieties and emotions that constitute the public temper in regard to crime. People look to criminal justice not just for an efficient dispatching of the individual offender but also as symbolic reassertions of order and authority which help them deal with their feelings of helplessness, disorder and insecurity. But Durkheim is wrong to take it for granted that these rituals will always "work" in this socially functional manner. In fact, the success of the penal process will depend not just upon the justice of the particular case, but also, and crucially, upon the coherence or diversity of the social order which surrounds it.

Wherever a community is not completely homogeneous — which is to say virtually everywhere — there will tend to be different audiences for such public ceremonies and different responses to it. Some onlookers will experience recognition, identity, and reinforcement of faith, while for others the ceremony may reveal raw coercion rather than authority, an alien power rather than a shared belief. The result may sometimes be the social cohesion that Durkheim assumes, but it may equally be a recharging of social divisions and the inflaming of hostile enmities between different groups.

The recent New York cases such as the B. Goetz case or the Jogger in the Park illustrate my point. Durkheim is right to argue that criminal cases become the focus for social anxieties, moral and political beliefs, and passionate feelings, but because his focus is upon the interaction between society and the individual, and not the relations between mutually warring groups, he fails to see how such trials can pull societies apart as well as hold them together. (The trials of the LAPD officers in the Rodney King case, the case of Reginald Denny, and of O.J. Simpson show up racial divisions in the USA, in the same way that the acquittal of Austin Donnellin showed up sexual divisions in the UK). As George Herbert Mead (1918) points out, the sentiments of solidarity evoked by the criminal trial are sentiments of hostility against a perceived enemy. And when that enemy takes a group form, rather than an individual one, it is a recipe for intolerance and escalating division rather than societal integration.

Repressive and restitutive sanctions

Durkheim's classification of laws and sanctions in the two categories of "repressive law" (which embodies the shared values of mechanical solidarity) and "restitutive law" (which expresses and restores relationships of organic solidarity) is also problematic. It is, of course, a sociological classification of laws rather than a legal one — lawyers wouldn't recognise it — and if it is to continue to be useful, we need to adapt it to the changing forms of modern law, rather than accept Durkheim's exposition, which correlates "repressive law" with the whole of criminal (or penal) law, and "restitutive law" with the remainder ("civil law, commercial law, procedural law, administrative and constitutional law...," [1893b] 1933b: 69).

I would argue that much contemporary penal law and practice exhibit a restitutive rather than a repressive character, being concerned to restore the *status quo ante* and compensate injured parties, rather than to reassert a shared moral code through punishment. Thus if one thinks of the extensive use now made of compensation orders, cautions, diversion from prosecution, and reparation and mediation, it becomes apparent that penal law is no longer straightforwardly "repressive" in Durkheim's sense.

Indeed, the vast bulk of criminal sanctions — which today are mainly fines, fixed penalties, community service orders and probation (even when we leave road traffic offences out of account) — do not seem to fit Durkheim's description of a repressive law expressing mechanical solidarity. Fines and community measures carry little moral weight and are not given much publicity. There is little "disgrace" involved, little "passion". Above all, there is no real sense of the avenging of sacred transcendental deities (whether God or Society). On the contrary, they are mundane, routine, and regularly involve profane elements such as negotiating time to pay, instalment payments, and means tests.

Increasingly too, the victim is being brought into this process, and given a role in the proceedings, so that many crimes are dealt with as if they are a private matter between two parties, rather than a violation of public codes which must be avenged. All of this — as well as the tendency of recent policy to "define deviance down" through diversion from prosecution, fixed penalties, the *de facto* decriminalisation of much offending behaviour, and the state's attempt to persuade private organisations and communities to "take responsibility" for dealing with crime in their locale — is very much what one would expect in a modern, differentiated society, based upon interdependence, moral particularism, and organic solidarity. But to make such a broadly Durkheimian analysis we have to rethink Durkheim's legal concepts.

Penality today, then, blurs the boundaries which Durkheim sets up with his dichotomy of repressive and restitutive law. But he is certainly right to observe that modern societies still display elements of mechanical solidarity and still resort to repressive punitive rituals, albeit for a narrower range of conducts. The public condemnation and punishment of anathematised individuals is still very much a characteristic of contemporary society, though these must be seen as strategies of rule as much as expressions of public sentiment (cf. Foucault's analysis in *Discipline and Punish)*. Nevertheless, it is notable that the offences and offenders which are singled out for this archaic ritual are generally those whose behaviour appears to threaten the values and sentiments of tightly knit and solidaristic social units (such as families, local communities, etc.) rather than those which do harm to the "organic" social fabric of the wider society. For example, it seems unlikely that the perpetrator of the criminal fraud which led to the recent collapse of the Barings securities firm will be sentenced to a very lengthy prison sentence, despite the damage that this financial catastrophe inflicted upon the global markets and hence the interdependent lives of each of us.

David Garland

REFERENCES

References to Durkheim follow the system initiated by Lukes: see Foreword

Bartlett, R. 1986. *Trial by Fire and Water.* Oxford: OUP.

Dahrendorf R. 1985. *Law and Order.* London: Stevens.

Durkheim, E. [1893b] 1933b. *The Division of Labour in Society.* New York: Macmillan.

Durkheim, E. [1901a (i)] 1973b. "Two Laws of Penal Evolution", in S. Lukes and A. Scull, eds., *Durkheim and the Law.* London: M. Robertson.

Durkheim, E. [1925a] 1961a. *Moral Education.* New York: Free Press.

Durkheim, E. [1950a] 1957a. *Professional Ethics and Civic Morals.* London: Routledge.

Foucault, M. 1977a. *Discipline and Punish.* London: Allen Lane.

Garland, D. 1990. *Punishment and Modern Society.* Oxford: Clarendon Press.

Gatrell, V. A. C., B. Lenman and G. Parker. 1980. *Crime and the Law: The Social History of Crime in Western Europe since 1500.* London: Europa.

Geertz, C. 1983. "Centers, Kings and Charisma: Reflections on the Symbolics of Power", in C. Geertz, *Local Knowledge.* New York: Basic Books.

Hunt, L. 1988. "The Sacred and the French Revolution" in J. Alexander, ed., *Durkheimian Sociology: Cultural Studies*, Cambridge: CUP.

Malinowski, B. 1926. *Crime and Custom in Savage Society.* London: Heinemann.

Mauss, M. 1967. *The Gift.* London: Routledge & Kegan Paul.

Mead, G. H. 1918. "The Psychology of Punitive Justice", *American Journal of Sociology* 23: 577–602.

Schwartz, R.D. and J. C. Miller. 1964. "Legal Evolution and Societal Complexity", *American Journal of Sociology* 70, 159–169.

Selznick, P. 1993. *The Moral Commonwealth.* Berkeley: University of California Press.

Shils, E. 1982. *The Constitution of Society.* Chicago: University of Chicago Press.

Smith, A. 1976. *The Theory of Moral Sentiments.* Oxford: OUP.

Spitzer, S. 1975. "Punishment and Social Organisation", *Law and Society Review* 9: 613–637.

Weber, M. 1978. *Economy and Society*, 2 vols., edited by G. Roth and C. Wittich. Berkeley: University of California Press.

Wrong, D. 1994. *The Problem of Order.* New York: Free Press.

Chapter Three

THE ADMINISTRATION OF PUNISHMENT IN SCHOOLS

W. S. F. Pickering

Introduction

In Durkheim's eyes reasons for punishment have to be gleaned from the basic values — from the *représentations collectives* — of the society in which the punishment is carried out. Reasons for punishment are therefore unlikely to be universal and should never be seen in the abstract. Initially all reasons or "theories" are relativist.

When Durkheim dealt with punishment in schools, as he did surprisingly extensively in lectures he began to deliver in 1898 in Bordeaux and which were published in 1925 as *L'Education morale* (1925a), he considered such punishment, not in abstraction, but strictly within the milieu of the school in late nineteenth-century France. Inevitably he could not avoid questions of a wider kind.

In this short exposition of Durkheim's position over corporal punishment, I adopt a procedure which is the reverse of the one which was taken by Durkheim himself. I start with practice and then relate it to theory. This procedure is not as irrational as might appear. Parents are sometimes known to administer punishment and later reflect on what they have done and why they have done it. Admittedly it is a method of procedure which Durkheim, as we shall see, strongly criticised.

1 Undesirable practice

Physical punishment

Durkheim stood totally opposed to the use of corporal punishment in schools (1925a: 224/t.1961a: 197). He was adamant
that it should be completely prohibited and he was delighted that
it had been eliminated in all French public schools. Why was
this?

Physical punishment, Durkheim held, injured a child's health,
and he implied both a child's moral and physical health (ibid.:
224/197).[1] Very simply he took the position that such punishment
is dehumanizing. He stated categorically: "In beating, in brutality
of all kinds, there is something we find repugnant, something
which shocks (*révolter*) our conscience, in a word, something
immoral" (208/183). Again, "all violence exercised on a person
seems to us in principle like sacrilege" (ibid.). And Durkheim
goes beyond the issue of a child and applies it to an adult as well.
To paraphrase Durkheim we may say that when we corporally
punish an adult we view the person no longer as a human being
but as an animal or object. In this way we put an offender outside
the human family (ibid.).

But not only does physical violence in schools shock us, it is
also counterproductive. And for this reason. The chief object of
moral education is to instil in the child a humanistic morality —
to give the child "a feeling of the dignity of man" (ibid.). Physical
punishment is the very denial of such dignity. The morality it en-
genders is one of brutality, which is no morality.

However, there is an exception which Durkheim maintains
does not undermine his humanistic approach. Corporal punishment is justifiable while the child is still "a small animal" (*un
petit animal*) (209/183). Here the issue is one of training
(*dressage*, as in the breaking in of a horse). This should occur

only in the home and never in the school, for in the home physical punishment is softened by tenderness, or should be. The pain is ameliorated by the intimacy of parental affection. Contrast this with a school where punishment has to be administered impersonally. *Ergo*, corporal punishment should be totally absent in all teaching institutions.

Here Durkheim sees a significant difference between the process of training young children and educating them. For an animal, and hence for a very young child, the main — sometimes the only effective method is where pain is inflicted. For a creature, be it an animal or child, learning by the senses is the only way to achieve the goal. For the older child, pain, if any is inflicted, is only a symbol which impinges on the inner state of the child.

From this position — and I focus solely on the rejection of physical punishment in the process of education — two questions arise. One, why should Durkheim be such a strong advocate of the rejection of physical punishment in schools, which seems so contrary to the practice say, of the English at the time? And two, how did he account for variations over time in the use of physical punishment in schools?

Durkheim's humanism

It has just been shown that Durkheim offered various reasons for his rejection of physical punishment in schools and such reasons stem from his basic ideological outlook, that of a convinced and devoted humanist. His attitude to corporal punishment was not unique or original: he merely supported and reflected a popular movement in France which in many respects was epitomised in the policy of the Third Republic, and which was based on a secular, humanist morality, which is generally referred to as *la morale laïque.* Given the fact that, as Durkheim argues, corporal punishment degrades the person, it cannot be viewed in any other way than in being a denial of a morality based on the sacredness of the person. In the eyes of the humanist of the times, no punishment can be worse than physical punishment, whether it is administered in the school or in adult society. Beatings, floggings, mutilations, branding, sending criminals to the galleys, and torture were so terrible that no man or woman, let alone a child, irrespective of the crime or offence, should ever have to endure them. For adults, imprisonment, irrespective of the length of time served, was the acceptable, humane way of dealing with offenders. Humanism is quintessentially a movement for the alleviation of human suffering, and the most obvious form, which can be relatively easily relieved, is physical suffering. As we have hinted, the individual in Durkheim's view is held to be sacred: one does not mutilate the sacred, for that is an act of profanation.

Another reason might be seen in the policy of the Third Republic in radically reforming the school system of which one aspect was the continued abolition of corporal punishment. From this, it can be argued that, as we have asserted, all that Durkheim did, as a teacher of education in the university, was a mere echo of the prevailing ideology. Of course, he was not obliged to take this line and he was not uncritical of the state of French society or of its educational system, for he deeply desired change, for example in the inheritance laws and in the creation of a healthy, just society, but it is true he never favoured anything approaching a revolution. One sees, however, that when he writes about the complete undesirability of corporal punishment, he does so, not because politically he felt obliged to, but from the depth of his heart.

A third reason might be tentatively raised. This centres on Durkheim's Jewish background. Did his attitude towards corporal punishment spring from such origins? This is a complex question but the answer seems to be a firm no. In Jewish homes children's good deeds were rewarded positively and children were firmly talked to when they misbehaved. Sometimes children were sent to their rooms and had to eat alone, that is, punishment was by isolation.[2] Yet it is unlikely that in the matter of corporal punishment, there was any serious difference between Jewish and gentile households in France, except perhaps in Catholic right-wing circles. Early Jewish thought certainly recommended corporal punishment. One reads in Proverbs "the rod and reproof give wisdom; but a child left to himself bringeth his mother to shame" (ch.29, v.15).[3] Perhaps on this proverb, the common English adage, "spare the rod and spoil the child" was built.[4]

Seeking an explanation of the use of corporal punishment in the past

Durkheim sets out to enquire why western societies until fairly recently have either seen the need to punish children physically, or held it to be desirable.

Contrary to what one might think, Durkheim argued that pre-literate societies, even in those which are generally held to be cruel, children are gently disciplined. One outstanding example is that of the aboriginal Indians in North and South America where children are very affectionately treated. Durkheim held that in an examination of 104 primitive societies, as he and others then called them, only 13 had an education which could be called severe (210/184).

It was his contention that severity of punishment in schools in the western world came with the establishment of monasteries when the rod and fasting were widely applied to children. He noted that the severities were less at the beginning of the Middle Ages than at the end.

But Durkheim does not find this argument in itself to be completely satisfying. The question arises, why should the development

43

of European civilization into the Middle Ages and beyond have been accompanied by school "malpractices" which are nothing short of dehumanizing? One must look at society in a wider sweep.

He produced arguments which are not dissimilar to those of the *Division of Labour* (1893b) and "The Two Laws of Penal Evolution" (1901a(i)) in which he tries to account for historical changes in attitudes to punishment. In *L'Education morale* he states that in preliterate societies life is simple, based on a few uncomplicated ideas, where occupations and work are not clearly differentiated (1925a: 215/189). Education for the child is therefore correspondingly simple: indeed, education in our general sense of the word is virtually absent. The child readily learns through experience, though elders may see fit to intervene in the process.

As cultures become more complex, coupled with an increased division of labour, so does education itself and one result is severer punishment meted out to children. Durkheim admits this is a rather naïve position to adopt and one might add, is by itself contrary to his argument in the *Division of Labour*, and "Two Laws of Penal Evolution" where he asserts that as society becomes more complex so attitudes towards punishment tend to become less severe and more humane. Thus, the moral conscience becomes progressively refined, manners become milder and violence increasingly repugnant.

Durkheim's explanation is unconvincing in another way. It does not explain why there should be a cruel system of school punishment in the Middle Ages when civilization was at a fairly high level and when the philosophy of the day had reached such a high level of sophistication. Perhaps the cruelty is more due to basic Christian doctrines about man and the evils of the flesh than Durkheim was prepared to admit. However, Philippe Ariès in *L'Enfant et la vie familiale sous l'ancien régime* has noted that although the birch was a much used instrument of punishment in medieval schools, it was the poorer students who suffered most, since the birch was sometimes used as a substitute for fines (Ariès [1960] 1962: 259).

Durkheim uses a further argument that medieval schools were organised in such a way that public opinion had no chance of penetrating them. They were closed societies like the guilds. The danger always is that such societies all too readily degenerate into despotism. It was public opinion against severe corporal punishment that eventually caused it to be phased out in France in the late eighteenth century. But this issue Durkheim does not raise when offering a detailed account of why corporal punishment declined in schools in France over the past two hundred years or so. Nor does he attempt to note the remarkable difference in the practice between France and Britain from the late eighteenth century onwards. Of course we should not criticise Durkheim for doing something he did not intend to do. In his book on suicide he was happy to make comparisons (1897a). According to Ariès, corporal punishment in schools in France was eliminated in around 1763 with the expulsion of the Jesuits who had been supporters of punishment (Ariès 1962: 262ff.). The struggle to abolish physical punishment was successful despite opposition in some church circles. In England, however, notwithstanding a growing humanism, violence and brutality persisted in eighteenth century schools. Although Arnold of Rugby later attempted to bring about moderation in floggings in public and other schools, the educational maxim prevailed: a good beating was "an opportunity for the boy being flogged to exercise self-control, the first duty of the English gentleman" (quoted in Aries 1962: 264). One might add that unlike France again, flogging for adults in England, Prussia, and Russia extended well into the nineteenth century.

2 Desirable practice

What form of punishment?

Having rejected corporal punishment for school children, what form of punishment did Durkheim hold to be legitimate? Deprivation was the answer. The child should be forbidden to participate in games and be made to feel contrite in the face of an offence (225/197). Punishment should be useful (*servir*) and of service to the child. This is not far from the notion of rehabilitation, which Durkheim felt was the correct principle for punishing adults. As such it is motivated by humanitarian sentiments.

Along these lines, however, Durkheim rejected certain school punishments, such as dull copying, e.g. writing out lines and forcing children to do tedious chores. To exert educational influence, punishment must be seen to produce attitudes of respect in the offender. School impositions are hardly likely to produce this. Punishment by way of supplementary tasks seems satisfactory but it should have the same characteristics as general tasks. The offender has to do more of the ordinary and, therefore, embark on positive work within the school.

Durkheim was also against group punishment in which all offenders are punished together (226/198). This creates hostility amongst members of the group and therefore increases mutual damage. He was also against group punishment in prisons.

In the type of punishment that Durkheim advocated in forbidding offenders to take part in games or giving them extra positive tasks coupled with reproach and reprimand, one thing is necessary — a graduated scale of punishment. Such a scale begins as low as possible and care has to be shown to the offender that he is moving from one scale to another.

Continual punishment

Punishment loses its effectiveness, says Durkheim, every time it is applied. Therefore, too constricted a scale of punishments is dangerous since it is soon exhausted for persistent offenders. The threat-value deteriorates quickly. In this lies the weakness of Draconian laws. Such measures move immediately to harshness and become ineffective. The effectiveness of punishment declines with the frequency of application. There emerges a point of no return where increased punishment produces no useful effect at all (228/200). Punishment, then, should not be administered in massive doses. All punishment must be preceded by a warning, reproach or disapproval — by a glance, a gesture, or silence (227/199).

The issue of time

The teacher or parent must never strike a child, and most certainly never strike a child in anger. This is clearly compatible with traditional rational thinking. An impulsive response to an offence deprives the action of all moral significance. Thus, a little time should elapse between the act of offence and punishment. For adults the judiciary system with its slowness and complications guarantees that an adequate time intervenes between offence and punishment. The teacher should always be sensitive and reflective about the punishment he metes out to the offending child.

Durkheim held that there were and must be differences in the administration of punishment in a school and in society at large — in the adult world. One difference rests with the particular nature of a school class and the schoolroom which is not a copy of society, although the class should be viewed as a collectivity (231/203). The offences in the schoolroom are usually clear to see and are immediate. The child is caught in an act of misbehaviour. There is no doubt about the facts of the case and there are no complicated trial procedures (ibid.). This affects the time span between the wrongful act and the infliction of punishment which Durkheim saw was of crucial importance in dealing with children. A long delay in punishment is counterproductive. It is desirable that the effect of the misdeed is nullified as soon as possible.

The family should never hand over to the school its own authority, since it is not an extension of the family. But neither is it an extension of society (see below). The school is very much an institution in its own right and therefore has to be treated sociologically as such. One consequence is that the parents under normal circumstances cannot perform the function of a school. Hence every child should attend school.

Durkheim showed great sensitivity in the administration of punishment which we hope were reflected in his role as father of Marie and André. Good judgment based on sound reasoning should permeate the actions of judges and magistrates on the one hand, and school teachers on the other. Durkheim's sensitivity and perhaps anguish are shown when he wrote: "It is always something of a problem to know whether one should punish, and above all how to do it" (229/201). But something is quite clear: to achieve a given aim, only a minimum of punishment should be meted out. If anger in punishment be deplored, so also should be coldness and dispassion. Punishment should always be accompanied by revulsion, as in the common English supposedly mouthed by teacher or parent "This will hurt me more than it hurts you" (ibid.).

The issue is passion associated with suffering (230ff./202ff.). Excessive coldness or impassivity must be avoided. Punishment must demonstrate the revulsion the person administering punishment feels. Should all emotion be drained from it, the moral content is eliminated and it becomes a sheer physical act. In this way it is not educative. A child cannot accept useless punishment or punishment that does not have a *raison d'être*. In his notes on Rousseau and education, Durkheim emphasised: "Children should never receive punishment as such; it should always come as the natural consequence of their fault" ([1919a] 1979a: 177). So punishment is to be seen as a "natural" consequence of an immoral act. But in what way natural? A simple cause and effect? But surely only according to social determinants?

Role of rewards in education

Rewards in school should be used for "means of stimulating qualities of intelligence rather than those of the heart and character" (232/204). Durkheim sees that intellectual failure or success is qualitatively different from moral failure or "success". While it would be desirable to have a system of rewards for good moral behaviour, this is virtually impossible in practice to bring about. "Reward is an instrument of intellectual culture rather than moral culture" (ibid.). This would seem to disadvantage moral education at the expense of intellectual education because moral deeds are difficult to define and cannot be positively rewarded. Such is the argument of Durkheim.

3 Theories of punishment

Theories rejected: prevention

Some punishment is necessary but for what purpose? Durkheim appears to have been dissatisfied with all the theories of punishment which could in any way be held to be applicable to schools.

In such a context, he rejected outright several traditional theories of punishment, not least that of prevention. He admitted that the fear of punishment could be effective among some people (184/161). But it is neither the sole nor even chief reason for punishment. Such reasons are of secondary importance. In itself prevention fails to elicit moral change in the offender. Intimidation does not necessarily make for moral change. Italian studies had claimed that the prophylactic influence of punishment had been exaggerated. Danger, which is allied to fear and carries with it the possibility of suffering, does not deter people working in hazardous industries, for example, in the mines. Nor does it deter deep sea fishermen, and we might add, soldiers (185/162). Indeed, argued Durkheim, these people love such occupations. Those who have a sense of calling are not prevented by the hazards that it entails. But how far can it be said that those who work in mines, those who are soldiers and, we could add, robbers, have a vocation to such work? Most people in these occupations, it can be argued, have no alternative, since there is no real possibility of other work.

The limitation of the prevention theory also applies to the classroom. Physical punishments in themselves probably do not prevent immoral actions, for they do not create a sense of morality. In fact they may elicit bad feelings in a child.

In this respect Durkheim was opposed to the notion that punishment in general should be seen as a "natural" process, that is, that a misdemeanour has natural consequences in the form of punishment (192ff./168ff.). Rousseau is accredited with such a notion, and indeed held that punishment should not be inflicted, but it was applicable to a child, only to the age of twelve. For him, moral life begins at this age. Up to that time, the child, like an animal, lives a purely physical life. One sees perhaps the influence of Rousseau on Durkheim, for as has been noted, Durkheim advocated physical punishment only for very young children. As soon as moral education begins, the teacher must intervene and therefore point the child to moral precepts.

It is generally agreed that the punishment should fit the crime in adult and in school life. But in the way punishment is administered, there is a ready acceptance of equivalent sanctions of unequal offences. If, however, punishment is to forestall a forbidden act it should not relate to the nature of that act but to the intensity or strength of the inclination to commit the act. This means, therefore, that a prevention theory is at variance with the notion that the punishment should fit the crime (186/163).

The theory of expurgation or expiation rejected?

The theory of atonement or expiation as the reason for punishment has had a long history. The argument is that compensation has to be made for what has been done. The atonement annuls the evil that the offender has committed. The offender has to undergo punishment in order to eliminate the evil he or she has committed.

To some, Durkheim held, the notion is absurd and irrational (188/164). In what way can the evil of punishment inflicted on an offender compensate for the evil he or she has done to another person? Durkheim's humanism again becomes apparent in his assertion that all suffering is evil. Expiation is based on the notion of retaliation (ibid.). To most humanistic thinkers such assumptions and assertions are totally unacceptable.

Durkheim, however, is cautious. He holds that there is something of this theory that should be retained, namely, that punishment erases or makes amends. It is not a question that the offender has to undergo moral purgation, or that he or she is receiving just deserts. The actual suffering is far less significant that we imagine. What is necessary is that the punishment must demonstrate that an offence produces a moral wrong which must be negated or expurgated (189/165).

At this point we come face to face with certain aspects of Durkheim's notion of morality.

Moral authority rests on opinion, that is peoples' attitudes towards morality. In schools, Durkheim argues, children should have a feeling for the sacred and its inviolable nature, which stands totally outside their control (189/165). An act of delinquency is a violation of the rule. It means that the moral rule loses its sacredness. Thus, a violation undermines a child's faith in the intangible — might one say the transcendental quality of a rule. A child submits to the rule because the child sees the rule is endowed with a prestige, which is shattered when people disregard it. This demoralization continues if no action is taken against the offender. In short, it weakens the sacred authority of the rule. It is necessary, then, to demonstrate the strength of reversal, proportional to the attack made against the rule. "Punishment is nothing but this meaningful demonstration" (190/166).

The reaction against the offence and the affirmation of the sacred quality of the rule is mediated through the teacher. The child respects the rule because she or he has faith in the teacher. If the teacher allows the violation of the rule, the child respects neither the teacher nor the rule. The teacher must punish and demonstrate unequivocally that he or she is committed to the rule despite the offence. The rule is the rule and must be obeyed (191/167).

One can conclude therefore that punishment is not for expiation undergone by the offender who does not have to nullify any guilt but rather is carried out to reassure and strengthen consciences. A violation of the rule can and must disturb people's faith, "even though they themselves cannot give an account of it" (ibid.). Discipline, then, plays an important part in the function of strengthening the morality of the school. Punishment prevents discipline from losing its authority. What is important is not that the child should suffer but that his behaviour should be vigorously censored. Punishment is disapproval shown against a given conduct. Durkheim hopes in this way that the offender will be educated morally because that is really what education is all about.

The principle

Punishment for offences by children is to be seen in the light of the process of education (230/202). The purpose of education is to prepare the child for adult life and to embrace the civilization in which the child is born, but that means that education must produce lasting, inner effects on the moral development of the child.

Durkheim's concept and function of punishment as part of that education is based on his psychology of the child and on his own humanistic ideology, which he saw as that which existed in France (149ff./129ff.). He combined fact with the desirable: in his day such a combination which seemed easy to achieve.

But at the basis of this stood the premise that the child needed to be taught moderation and self-control and to be shown categorically that there are limitations to his or her needs. "It [education] suffices to lead the child to acquire regular habits with respect to everything which bears on its life" (157/138).

Durkheim distinguished respect for rule and authority, which is held to be good, from the fear of punishment, which is bad (199/174). The clearest way of showing disapproval and upholding the sacred rule is to make the offender suffer. There is only one way of showing that one disapproves of someone and that is to treat him or her less well than people one esteems (191/167).

But let it be clearly understood that pain is incidental to the punishment, not its essential element. It is a sign *(signe)* by which the sentiment translates itself externally — a sentiment which needs to be informed and reformed in the face of the fault. It is the sentiment expressed, not the sign by which it is expressed, that neutralises the morally disruptive effect of the violation.

Thus, for Durkheim, school punishment and discipline are a means of restoring moral credibility, of upholding the moral system and communicating moral truth. In the words of David Garland punishment is seen by Durkheim to be a "social necessity" (Garland 1990: 58). This social necessity is obviously related directly to his concept of society.

And so the purpose of punishment in schools and one might add, adult life, is to restore the damage done to the sacred moral system and negate the profanation created by an immoral act. The system has to continue intact, with its authority fully restored and so guarantees the persistence of society. Whether punishment really achieves that is open to debate. And, further, there are some who would not equate a moral system, let alone a legal one, with the sacred, indeed the concept of the sacred is not part of a secular society(see Pickering 1990).

And now?

We have briefly stated Durkheim's position about punishment in schools. Where is its relevance today? Despite some of the obvious weaknesses of his argument, not least about the sacredness of the person, and his assumption about the evil of corporal punishment on the individual, the battle seems to have been won. Corporal punishment in state schools in Europe and elsewhere is prohibited, even in a slow moving country like Britain. But there are two merits in examining Durkheim's arguments. First, they are a closely reasoned and admirable statement, despite some flaws, for the non-application of corporal punishment in schools and indeed in society at large. Second, although victory seems assured, those calling for the restoration of physical punishment are always lurking in the wings, for example in the United States and in parts of Europe.[5] And one should be aware of the fact that in Britain corporal punishment is still permitted in private schools, even though it is said it is seldom administered. Any threat on the part of those such advocating such punishment needs to be firmly met and Durkheim's gambit is perhaps the most powerful we have.

NOTES

1. References in brackets which contain no key date, relate to *L'Education morale* (1925a). The first number refers to the French text, the second refers to the corresponding page number of the English translation of 1961a.

2. A male descendant of the Durkheim family told me that he did not think there was any difference in the use of use of corporal punishment between Jewish and gentile families in France. Sometimes the cane was given in home on the hand, never on the buttocks. When he was about eleven years of age punishment was in the form of being sent to one's room and not having meals with one's parents. Such isolation as punishment is rejected by the Hutterites, an Anabaptist sect, where the strap and the cane are used and the child is then embraced by the administrator.

3. I have been told that there exists a late medieval picture of a Jewish boy being beaten.

4. The United Kingdom has shown itself to be one of the last countries in the Western world to abolish physical punishment in schools. Writing in the early 1970s, Newell noted that in Europe at that time, the only countries which gave the right to use corporal punishment

were the United Kingdom, Eire, some Cantons in Switzerland, and in certain Länder in Germany (Newell 1972: 9–10). Countries colonised by Britain also tended to allow physical punishment in schools. In Britain itself, the practice was used less and less in the years that followed the Second World War. Often it was the teachers who opposed its abolition (ibid.: 175) and recommendations for abolition were frequently disregarded by the government of the day. The Society of Teachers Opposed to Physical Punishment was active in the 1960s and early 1970s and helped to bring about the abolition of corporal punishment. It was not until August 1986 that an act of Parliament finally brought to an end to such punishment in state schools.

5. Some British parents still demand the right to beat their children, admittedly in the home. As recently as November 1997 a case was heard on the subject before the European Commission on Human Rights which forced the British government to consider its position. The government decided not to ban corporal punishment altogether but to continue to allow parents the right of reasonable chastisement of their children (see *Guardian* 8 November 1997).

REFERENCES

References to Durkheim follow the system initiated by Lukes: see Foreword

Ariès, P. 1960. *L'Enfant et la familiale sous l'ancien régime.* Paris: Editions du Seuil
(1962. *Centuries of Childhood.* London: Jonathan Cape).
Durkheim, E. [1893b] 1902b. *De la Division du travail social,* 2nd edition. Paris: Alcan.
(1933b. *The Division of Labour in Society.* New York: Macmillan.)
Durkheim, E. 1897a. *Le Suicide: étude de sociologie.* Paris: Alcan.
(1951a. *Suicide: A Study in Sociology.* Glencoe, Ill.: Free Press).
Durkheim, E. 1901a (i). "Deux Lois de l'évolution pénale", *Année sociologique,* IV: 65–95.
(1969e. "Two Laws of Penal Evolution", *University of Cincinnati Law Review,* 38: 32–60).

Durkheim, E. 1919a. "La 'Pédagogie' de Rousseau", *Revue de métaphysique et de morale*, XXVI: 153–180.
(1979a. "Rousseau on Educational Theory", in W. S. F. Pickering, ed., *Durkheim: Essays on Morals and Education*. London: Routledge & Kegan Paul).

Durkheim, E. 1925a. *L'Education morale*, introduction by Paul Fauconnet, Paris: Alcan .
(1961a. *Moral Education*. New York: Free Press).

Garland, D. 1990. *Punishment and Modern Society: A Study in Social Theory*. Oxford: Clarendon Press.

Lukes, S. 1973. *Emile Durkheim, His Life and Work: A Historical and Critical Study*. London: Allen Lane. (New edition 1992, London: Penguin.)

Newell, P., ed. 1972. *A Last Resort? Corporate Punishment in Schools.* Harmondsworth: Penguin.

Pickering, W. S. F. 1990. "The Eternality of the Sacred: Durkheim's Error?", *Archives de sciences sociales des religions*, 69: 91–106.

Chapter Four

THE REALM OF NORMATIVITY IN DURKHEIM AND FOUCAULT

Werner Gephart

Introduction

Foucault's vision of the disciplinary society focuses on the following image: We live in a society of the judge-professor, the judge-physician, the judge-pedagogue, and the judge-social worker. These are the dominating figures in a new "realm", the realm of normativity. They all work for the realm of normativity; everybody there is subdued by one's body, gestures, behaviour, faculties and achievements. This is meant to expose the idea of the rule of law. Domination by law is not a pure cliché; it is rather a marking of class domination. Moreover, the rule of law has to be taken literally: the realm of normativity extends over the whole "social body" and the judge-professors, the judge-physicians, the judge-pedagogues are the administrators of that realm. The technocrats of the norm are at the same time the administrators of the normalising institutions, spreading the panopticon from a fictional centre to the entire society. The microphysics of power are transferred into the macrophysics of society, constituted through endless mechanisms of intertwined "disciplines". This, in a nut shell, is Foucault's negative utopia of the disciplinary society.

It seems like an elective affinity when Foucault does not deem any sociologist except Emile Durkheim to be worthy of citation (Foucault 1975: 28). That is why the question in my book concerning the analysis of "crime and punishment in Durkheim's theory of social life" (Gephart 1990) was directed to the *Durkheimian basis* in Foucault. In order to develop this interpretative hypothesis, I would here like to begin with a reconstruction of the place norms and normativity have in Durkheim's view of social life.

1 Emile Durkheim and the normative constitution of the world

The birth of sociology out of the spirit of law

Durkheim had given a confessional character to his understanding of the constitution of social life in the *Règles de la méthode sociologique*. Yet the title of Durkheim's *Rules* is revealing of the normative penetration of the world including the process of thought and science itself. It is not only the allusion to Descartes that makes him speak of the *Règles de la méthode sociologique*, but the deeply rooted conviction of the *normative* character of society. His academic career at Bordeaux starts with special reference to normative thinking, especially to law. There had been a dispute whether the "Cours de science sociale" would not have been better placed in the law faculty. As Durkheim stated: "Quand ce cours a eté créé, on s'est demandé si sa place n'était pas plutôt à l'Ecole de droit" (Durkheim [1888a] 1970a: 108).

Durkheim takes this dispute as an indicator of how much society and law, sociology and jurisprudence, are linked together: "C'est dans les entrailles même de la société que le droit s'élabore, et le législateur ne fait que consacrer un travail qui s'est fait sans lui" (ibid.: 108–109). On the other hand Durkheim views law as a relatively independent structure of society; twenty years later, in a debate about the reform of teaching law, he would exclaim: "Qu'on montre aux jeunes gens comment les institutions juridiques tiennent à des conditions sociales, varient avec ces conditions, sont solidaires des autres institutions, politiques, économiques, des idées morales, comment elle tiennent à la structure même des sociétés" (Durkheim [1907d] 1975b, vol. 1: 244). The rules of sociological method continue the line of the "Cours de science sociale" with a systematic foundation of sociology in the normative structuring of society.

It is in the postulates about the distinctive character of "social facts" that his normative and judicial orientation find expression. Yet the first example of a social fact is revealing and I quote the whole passage for a better understanding: "Quand je m'acquitte de ma tâche de frère, d'époux ou de citoyen, quand j'éxécute les engagements que j'ai contractés, je remplis des devoirs qui sont définis, en dehors de moi et de mes actes, dans le droit et dans les mœurs" (Durkheim [1901c] 1973: 3). This famous criterion of *exteriority* transmitted through law and customs at the same time exercises an external *constraint*: "Non seulement ces types de conduite ou de pensée sont extérieurs à l'individu, mais ils sont doués d'une *puissance impérative* et *coercitive* en vertu de laquelle ils s'imposent à lui, qu'il le veuille ou non" (ibid.: 4 — italics added).

This famous criterion of *constraint* paradigmatically fulfilled by judicial norms was debated in Parsons' view of Durkheim, where the "structure of social action" aimed to weaken the coercive character Durkheim ascribed to social life. But a comparative reading with Foucault once more demonstrates how radical Durkheim was in his theorising. Take for example one passage of an interview in 1975 with J. L. Ezine in *Les nouvelles littéraires* where the resemblance to Durkheim's definition of social fact is easily seen: "C'est la contrainte qui m'intéresse: comment elle pèse sur les consciences et s'inscrit dans le corps" (Foucault 1994, vol. 2: 723). Specialists familiar with Durkheim might oppose an identification of *law* and *social facts*, claiming that social facts belong to a group of phenomena less constituted by norms, namely "faits sociaux d'ordre anatomique ou morphologique". But, in fact, even in those morphological spheres, the primacy of law is penetrating: "C'est seulement à travers le droit public qu'il est possible d'étudier cette organisation, car c'est ce droit qui la détermine, tout comme il détermine nos relations domestiques et civiques" (Durkheim [1901c] 1973: 13). Again, the *normative constitution* of the social world dominates Durkheim's vision. Law, then, is a universal structure of social life, a privileged method which is in itself judicially formed. And even when the subject of knowledge is obliged to follow norms, that is, the rules of sociological method, Durkheim constructs a *realm of normativity*, from which nothing has a chance to escape.

The inherent tensions of normative systems

This picture of Durkheim's view on norms and normativity would be much too simple, if not simplistic, if the inherent tensions of normative systems were not taken into account. For the sake of a systematic interpretation, it is necessary to include the highly sophisticated model Durkheim developed about the plurality of normative systems.

In Durkheim's view, the types of different rules reflect the type of *sanction*. This is related to Durkheim's anti-naturalistic analysis of norms, as when he says: "La sanction ne tient donc pas à la nature intrinsèque de l'acte puisqu'elle peut disparaître, l'acte restant ce qu'il était" (Durkheim 1969g: 42). This view brings Durkheim close to the symbolic interactionist's point of view, namely, that the *sanction* defines the criminal: "Et voilà pourquoi c'est par elle (la sanction) que se définissent toutes les règles du droit et de la morale" (ibid.). On this basis Durkheim opens a normative space, built up along the lines of particularism and universalism as well as generalisation and individualisation.

All those norms referring to individual morality have the same degree of universalism as the so-called "morality of mankind", whereas domestic and civic ethics have a more concrete content, and professional ethics possesses a higher degree of particularism, because they regulate only the affairs of the professional group. We finally arrive at a rather consistent model of what I call the normative space or the realm of normativity which might be represented in the following way:

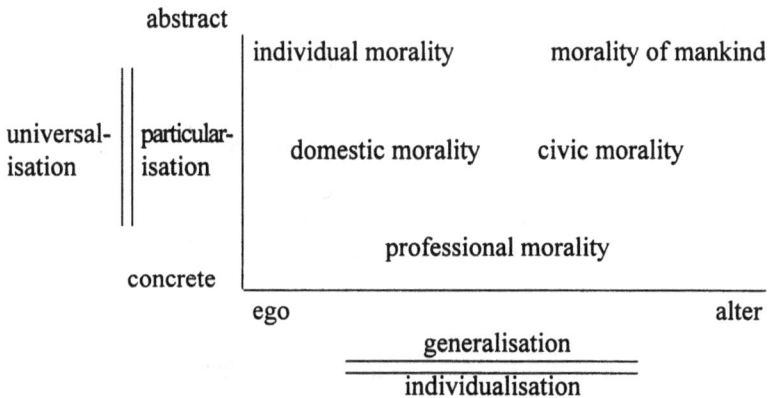

		abstract	
		individual morality	morality of mankind
universal-isation	particular-isation	domestic morality	civic morality
		professional morality	
	concrete		
	ego		alter
		generalisation	
		individualisation	

To support this interpretation, I would like to cite the following passage from the *Leçons de sociologie: physique des mœurs et du droit*, which goes as follows:

Ce particularisme morale, si l'on peut ainsi parler, qui est nul dans la morale individuelle, apparaît dans la morale domestique, pour atteindre son apogée dans la morale professionnelle, décliner avec la morale civique et disparaître à nouveau avec la morale qui règle les rapports des hommes en tant qu'hommes. (Durkheim 1969g: 45)

On a theoretical level, a model of differentiated encircling, or embracing, or "enfermement totale" has been developed. But it remains unclear what can hold together this *polymorphically overnormalized* society, for the conditions to generate valid norms differ between more concrete or more abstract norms especially when the normative structure of society is linked to its structuring principle, the mechanism of functional differentiation.

My argument, then, is that all the forms Durkheim treats as abnormal derivations of the division of labour, especially its anomic type, implicitly postulate the harmonious functioning of different normative systems. This possibility has led Durkheim — in my understanding — in the direction of a sacralisation of the realm of normativity which marks the kernel of his later "recherche du sacré perdu".

But how can we understand the role of crime and punishment from this ambivalent, normative construction of the world?

Crime and punishment in the circuit of collective feelings

After this reconstruction of a normative constitution of social life one would expect that crime would be interpreted as a break of norms and punishment as a more or less adequate reaction to it. Both expectations are false! Crime is defined as an attack on the conscience collective, which forms the basis of penal laws. The principle, "nul n'est censé d'ignoré la loi", is hinting at a sphere that needs special concretisation, for it is felt by everybody, the sphere being the "collective conscience" in the double meaning of the word: "...si les règles dont la peine punit la violation n'ont pas besoin de recevoir une expression juridique, c'est qu'elles ne sont l'object d'aucune contestation, c'est que tout le monde en sent l'autorité" (Durkheim [1893b] 1902b: 41).[1]

Crime is directed against the "conscience collective" and it unchains the collective feelings which need for their appearance a passionate reaction. That is why the punishment is logically bound to passions and collective feelings: "La peine consiste donc essentiellement dans une réaction passionelle" (ibid.: 64). Thus the emotive circuit being enforced by the crime is continued in the punitive reaction and thereby strengthens and stabilises the conscience collective. In this sense the crime is not in itself a pathological but a normal fact of social life, for it stabilises through punitive action the evolution of certain fields of the "conscience collective". Punishment does not have the effect of *special prevention* because the actor is not conceived as a rational being who makes choices between the various consequences of his action. Nor does it have a *general preventive* effect insofar as Durkheim does not believe in the force of deterrence for those who might be hindered from committing a crime.

And, finally, punishment does not belong to those *absolute theories* like those of Kant in which punishment enforces the normativity of norms. Durkheim's theory is stressing the latent function of punishment to conserve the *emotional basis* of social life. Crime and punishment, then, are like an endless wheel that keep the realm of normativity in motion.

Before moving on to Foucault I would like to draw your attention to the question of how Durkheim's view on religion might be included into this picture. It is perhaps not so well known that we can retrace the religious aspect of crime and punishment by way of a critique Marcel Mauss wrote on the book of Steinmetz, *Ethnologische Studien zur ersten Entwicklung der Strafe* (1882). This essay by Mauss was the brilliant start to a career which recently has been retraced by Michel Fournier. Durkheim himself found the essay so important that he devoted a *critique* to the *critique* of Mauss. What is the content of this dialogue? Durkheim made the following conclusion: "M. Mauss a su démêler dans le tabou l'institution religieuse d'ou dérive cette religiosité du droit pénale et nous croyons l'idée féconde" (Durkheim [1898a (iii) (13)] 1969c: 129).

First of all it is interesting to see how Mauss focuses on the *symbolic* level in his first publication when analysing social facts. "Private" vengeance is interpreted through the literal shedding of blood and its social meaning: "Mais le sang c'est ce qui est proprement commun à tout le clan, c'est sa vie" (Mauss [1896] 1969, vol. 2: 688). The conclusion is clear: "La solidarité religieuse du groupe, la sensibilité qu'il éprouve à *l'injure faite au sang*, sont donc la cause immédiate de la vengeance privée" (ibid.). But how is one to elucidate the religious origin of crime and punishment in a sphere not only of private but of public punishment: "C'est toujour la réaction diffuse du clan contre une insulte faite à des sentiments religieux, parce que ces sentiments forment le principe même de son existence morale...". Remaining in the stream of thought that Durkheim had opened with his emotive theory of punishment, Marcel Mauss lays down the *ambiguity* of the taboo and reveals the complexity of crime and punishment: "Le caractère ambigu des conséquences du tabou répond à sa nature même: il consilie le sacré et l'impur, il fait les dieux comme les criminels" (ibid.: 696).

We now have to consider a second figure of the *équipe* of the *Année sociologique*, one who continued Durkheim's rudimentary theory of crime and punishment. Paul Fauconnet had taken the responsibility for all those works to be critiqued on penal law in the *Année sociologique*. That is why we had no chance to learn from Durkheim himself what consequences the shift from law to religion might have had for his understanding of crime and punishment. But Fauconnet in his important and completely underestimated study, *La responsabilité* (1920), continued Durkheim's thought in examining the more difficult problem of how to interpret sociologically the judicial process of imputing an act to an actor who is to be treated as responsible. To quickly summarise a most complex book, the central idea is as follows: The object of punishment becomes a *symbolic* substitute of the violation of the collective sentiments, embodied by the criminal actor.

The realm of normativity, once more, is not that sphere of cold calculation — a utilitarian balancing of advantages and dis-advantages — but the sphere of collective feelings, the ambiguous attraction to and repulsion from taboo which make criminals like gods. In this sphere, punitive reaction is en-sconced in rites and collective festivities, because, more than the individual victim, it is society itself which has been violated.

Can Foucault be considered as one of the legitimate late mem-bers of the Durkheimian school in the France of the sixties and seventies?

2 Foucault's obsession with power and norms

Because Foucault's vision of the "naissance de la prison" has become quite familiar I need not repeat the scenes by which he wants to illustrate that *modern punishment* by imprisonment is even more cruel and inhuman than medieval practices of pun-ishment.

Although I think Foucault's reference to Durkheim in *Surveiller et punir* is revealing of his intellectual debt for his model of the normative constitution of social life,[2] I would like

67

to draw attention to another important source. In various interviews that are now posthumously collected as *Dits et écrits*, Foucault makes fun of those who look for the intellectual roots of an author, for example in his case, his Marxian roots. Of course, Marx is there and we will come to that. But more important and relevant are his affiliations with and admiration for Friedrich Nietzsche.

In an interview with J. J. Brochier, published in the magazine *Littéraire*, Foucault expresses his debts very clearly: "Maintenant je reste muet, quand il s'agit de Nietzsche. Du temps ou j'etais prof, j'ai souvent fait des cours sur lui, mais je ne le ferais plus aujourd'hui. Si j'étais prétentieux, je donnerais comme titre général à ce que je fais: généalogie de la morale" (Foucault 1994, vol. 2: 753). After this indication, it is interesting to note that we find the following in the "généalogie de la morale": "Sans cruauté, pas de fête: voilà ce qu'enseigne la plus ancienne et la plus longue histoire de l'homme — et dans le châtiment aussi il y a tant de fête!"

Concerning the Marxian basis in Foucault I think that his implicit abolitionist's point of view has a lot of to do with the utopia of a society free from normative regulation as we find in the young Marx of the Parisian manuscript. Law as an illusory concept of the dominating classes has to be unmasked in order to prepare a stateless society which has no other norms than those Habermas calls institutions. It is not surprising, then, to read in an interview about prisons and prison revolts the following: Foucault is asked, "Peut-on imaginer une société sans prison?" Foucault's response is, "Le problème en est de savoir si l'on peut imaginer une société dans laquelle l'application des règles serait contrôlée par les groupes eux-mêmes" (ibid.: 432).

As to the function of norms and sanctions, they have nothing to do with creating a material or formal justice, but rather they steer the system of *illegalities* around a normative complex allowing and legitimising certain acts and behaviour. The implementation of power and the legitimising of non-forbidden acts to a social class are some aspects we may add beyond the common reading of *Surveiller et punir*.

Conclusion

Between Durkheim and Foucault, the similarities and even elective affinities, if not historical debts, may be summarised as follows. Durkheim's solution to the problem of moral disorder in modern society, namely, a firmly constructed realm of normativity, is precisely the problem for Foucault. They coincide in that they give to constraint, (remember Foucault's, "c'est la contrainte qui m'intéresse", and Durkheim's definition of social facts), yet they differ in their evaluation of them. Power relations are underestimated in Durkheim, yet these are the main topic in Weber's thought. Indeed, the influence of Nietzsche unites Foucault and Weber for whom the notion of "discipline" is absolutely indispensable and equipped with a categorical methodological status. Moreover, it is clear that Durkheim raised the question of how to explain the "naissance de la prison" by referring to the evolution of power and domination. But what makes a lot of difference is the differing evaluation of *the facts*.

Once asked about the meaning of his writings, Foucault answered: "Je voudrais que mes livres soient des sortes de bistouris, de cocktails Molotov ou de galeries de mine, et qu'ils se carbonissent après usage à la manière de feux d'artifice."

Werner Gephart

NOTES

1. Followed by a footnote reference to Binding, *Die Normen und ihre Übertretung*.

2. For a detailed discussion, see Gephart 1990: 178–193.

REFERENCES

References to Durkheim follow the system initiated by Lukes: see Foreword

Durkheim, E. [1888a] 1970a. "Cours de science sociale. Leçon d'ouverture", in *La science sociale et l'action*, edited with introduction by J-C. Filloux. Paris: PUF.

Durkheim, E. [1893b] 1902b. *De la Division du travail social*, 2nd edition. Paris: Alcan.

Durkheim, E. [1898a (iii) (13)] 1969c. Review of Mauss, *La Religion et les origines du droit pénal*, in *Journal sociologique*, with introduction and notes by J. Duvignaud. Paris: PUF.

Durkheim, E. [1895a/1901c] 1973. *Les règles de la méthode sociologique*, 18th edition. Paris: PUF.

Durkheim, E. [1907d] 1975b. "Contribution à un débat de l'Union pour la vérité. Sur la réforme des institutions judiciares: l'enseignement du droit", in E. Durkheim, *Textes*, vol.1, edited by V. Karady. Paris: Editions de Minuit.

Durkheim, E. [1950a] 1969g. *Leçons de sociologie: physique des mœurs et du droit*, 2nd edition. Paris: PUF.

Fauconnet, P. 1920. *La responsabilité*. Paris: Alcan.

Foucault, M. 1975. *Surveiller et punir*. Paris: Gallimard.

Foucault, M. 1994. *Dits et écrits: 1954–1988*, vol.2. Paris: Gallimard.

Gephart, W. 1990. *Strafe und Verbrechen: die Theorie Emile Durkheims*. Opladen: Leske & Budrich.

Mauss, M. [1896] 1969. "La religion et les origines du droit pénal d'après un livre récent", in M. Mauss, *Œuvres*, vol.2, edited by V. Karady. Paris: Editions de Minuit.

Chapter Five

DURKHEIM AND FOUCAULT ON THE GENESIS OF THE DISCIPLINARY SOCIETY

William Ramp

1 An unlikely pairing

The idea of rereading Durkheim in light of Foucault, or of comparing the two, has drawn attention recently. Mike Gane calls *Discipline and Punish* a "delayed continuation of Durkheimian traditions" in the study of penal discipline, asserting that Foucault's "methodological fertility" owes a largely unmentioned debt to Durkheim (Gane 1992: 4; 1988: 182). Jeffrey Alexander links Foucault to Durkheim in a line of descent traced through 20th century linguistics and cultural anthropology (including Mauss, Saussure and Lévi-Strauss), noting that Foucault's work "rests on an intellectual base to which late Durkheimian thought made an indelible contribution" (Alexander 1988b: 6). But if Althusser, Lacan and even Foucault "acknowledged their debt" to Durkheim (Gane 1992: 5), Foucault did not emphasise it (Alexander 1988b: 6) as much as he did to Heidegger, Nietzsche, Weber, Husserl and the Frankfurt School (Foucault 1988b:145; 1993:18; Martin 1988: 12–13). Nor have Foucault's commentators made much of a Durkheim connection, stressing instead Foucault's reading of Nietzsche, Weber, Heidegger, Bachelard, Canguilhem, Dumézil, Lacan, Bataille and others (see, for example, Gutting 1989; Dreyfus and Rabinow 1983; Richman 1982: 72–75; Gordon 1993: 22–28; Pasquino 1993: 37–38, 40).

In one of Foucault's few references to Durkheim, in *Discipline and Punish*, he asks,

> But from what point can such a history of the modern soul on trial be written? If one confined oneself to the evolution of legislation or of penal procedures, one would run the risk of allowing a change in the collective sensibility, an increase in humanisation or the development of the human sciences to emerge as a massive, external, inert and primary fact. By studying only the general social forms, as Durkheim did..., one runs the risk of positing as the principle of greater leniency in punishment processes of individualisation that are rather one of the effects of the new tactics of power, among which are to be included the new penal mechanisms. (Foucault 1977a: 23)

Though Foucault ends up using something quite like a Durkheimian "symbolics of punishment", this single explicit reference to Durkheim is, as Gane puts it, "loftily dismissive" (1992: 26). Durkheim's fate in work by Foucault's contemporaries is generally similar: not praised or condemned, but mentioned only in passing, if at all.

This *lacuna* probably results from Durkheimianism's failure to become an accepted standard for the human sciences in France: Karady argues that even at their zenith, the Durkheimians were academically and socially marginalised (Karady 1981: 34–9; ibid. 1983; Weisz 1983), and despite Durkheim's wish to give sociology a disciplinary identity, the *Année sociologique* group did not develop a unitary research focus, a methodological or theoretical consensus, or close interpersonal ties. They were less a school than a work team (Besnard 1983b: 18). Losses in World War I weakened the group, and later its members (possibly excepting Halbwachs; see Craig 1983) specialised in distinctive areas without a metasociological agenda. Durkheim's own interest in a scientifically defensible moral foundation for the social life of the modern nation state was largely irrelevant to the moral concerns of French intellectuals and public figures by World War II (Karady 1983: 88), and some prominent Durkheimians refused to defend it in the educational battles of the 1920's (Geiger 1983: 130–131). Despite attempts between the wars to promote Durkheimianism as a standard of social-scientific orthodoxy, it did not become a clear target for potential enemies, and remaining members of the *Année* group pursued divergent interests without having to break with an official line. Durkheimianism crumbled without an Oedipal revolt, except perhaps against Durkheim's own tendency to metasociological abstraction and evolutionary optimism (a rejection echoing Durkheim's own critique of Comte).

But if no explicitly Durkheimian project survived Mauss's brief revival of the *Année*, it can be argued that Durkheimian theoretical, classificatory and substantive concerns continued to weave anonymously through French anthropological and cultural theory. In part, this may reflect Durkheim's appropriation of themes, topics and modes of analysis already present in French intellectual culture: he shared a disciplinary and political context with his opponents (Karady 1983). Still, a distinctively Durkheimian handling of such themes and modes of analysis became part of the intellectual heritage of French philosophy and the human sciences. Without an official label, however, it was neither attributed nor denied (Gane 1988: 182–3). Thus Foucault could dismiss Durkheim's work on penal discipline, yet exhibit features of a Durkheimian approach in his own studies. In light of such anomalies, certain thematic and other parallels between Durkheim and Foucault on the origins and nature of education, correctional discipline, and the development of the modern subject merit a second look; some might indicate linkages worth examining further. Here, however, I will focus mainly on the extent to which they might impel an ongoing revaluation of Durkheimian sociology.[1]

2 Methodological affinities

Althusser (1969) made a problematic attempt to establish a "fully positivized world view" for social science based on a "social ontology emancipated from all trace of ideological projection"; an exercise Wernick (1984: 143–5, 148 n. 27) calls part of a French "rationalist project", and which one might also term an attempt to read Marx through Comte. For Althusser, ideology was an invocation of a romanticised world in which subjects were constituted, located and called out, in relation to each other and to a generalised Subject, through forms of social practice. The ideological Subject appeared in many guises, including historical teleologies which located the present in a narrative continuity serving ideological ends. In a novel use of concepts of epistemological acts and thresholds (Bachelard), and displacements and transformations of concepts (Canguilhem), Althusser advocated an "epistemological break" by which such ideological continuities could be exposed to critical analysis.

Without reducing Foucault to Althusserianism, one can argue that he, too, subverted anthropocentric "histories of the present", suspending humanist continuities to trace the multiple, discontinuous and contradictory genesis of the present and its subjects. But Foucault's strategy in *The Archaeology of Knowledge* also had Durkheimian elements: like Durkheim, he rhetorically set up and destroyed received ideas about his subject matter, leading readers inexorably to an interrogation focused not on a hidden *telos* behind that subject matter, but on its actual, specific articulation. "Discourse," said Foucault, "must not be referred to the distant presence of the origin, but treated as and when it occurs" (Foucault 1972: 25). In contrast to received histories of thought:

> The analysis of the discursive field is orientated in a quite different way; we must grasp the statement in the exact specificity of its occurrence; determine its conditions of existence, fix at least its limits, establish its correlations with other statements that may be connected with it, and show what other forms of statement it excludes. We do not seek below what is manifest the half silent murmur of another discourse; we must show why it could not be other than what it was, in what respect it is exclusive of any other, how it assumes, in the midst of others and in relation to them, a place that no other could occupy. The question proper to such an analysis might be formulated in this way: what is this specific existence that emerges from what is said and nowhere else? (ibid.: 28)

This specificity is as true of the "gray, meticulous and patiently documentary" work of genealogy (Foucault 1977c) as of the archaeology described above. There is, in short, still a version of the Comtean distinction between "metaphysical" and "positive" forms of inquiry in Foucault (Martin 1988: 11; Patton 1979: 124, 127–30), as there was in Durkheim. Metaphysics takes for granted universal, self-sufficient and self-evident categories in explaining social and personal life. A positive approach maps specific events, practices, statements and techniques constitutive of such categories and subsequently forgotten; for example, the surveillance, confessional and classificatory practices constitutive of "sexuality" as a key feature of modern human life.

Durkheim, too, had continued the Comtean project (against Comte in a sense; see Durkheim [1900b] 1973a; Wernick 1984;

Meštrovic 1988), breaking with metaphysics to constitute sociology as a "positive", though not positivist (Meštrovic 1988) science. Just as Foucault claimed that nothing lay "behind" discursive practices, and that they had to be examined in their own right (not as mere products of authors or subjective agents), so Durkheim insisted on the *sui generis* existence of social facts, and on the replacement of generalisations with detailed empirical study resting on rationalist foundations and incorporating a necessary element of analytic abstraction (Meštrovic 1988; Jones and Kibbee 1993). Like Foucault, Durkheim abjured simplistic subject-object dualisms, refusing to reduce the social either to its agents or to its objective structures, and focused instead on collective representations, in their own specific articulation, as definitive of the social (Durkheim [1924a] 1974a: 1–34; Meštrovic 1988: 41–43). He interrogated the apparent universality of the category of property, locating its origins in specific family forms (Durkheim [1950a] 1957a), rooted logical categories in specific types of social organisation (Durkheim and Mauss [1903a(i)] 1963b), and examined religion not as the expression of a metaphysical unity, but as a concatenation of specific beliefs and rites. It is ironic that Foucault labelled Durkheim's analysis of penal discipline a Whig view of history trading on a meta-narrative about the evolution of leniency and neglecting the specific reorganisation of power and knowledge which gave rise to the modern individualised subject. The irony is deepened by the fact that both Durkheim and Foucault deliberately transgressed disciplinary boundaries in their investigations: despite their dedication to establishing sociology as a discipline, the Durkheimians showed in practice a similar tendency to ignore traditional disciplinary and topical borders in pursuit of the various dimensions of social phenomena (Karady 1983).

3 The rise of the "individual": governance and the disciplined subject

There are also substantive parallels between Durkheim's and Foucault's accounts of the emergence of modern pedagogy, governance and the individual subject. These have been eclipsed by similarities between Foucault's work on self-discipline and Weber's analysis of modern asceticism (e.g., O'Neill 1986); Weber's approach also appears more in line with Foucault's critical scepticism. Durkheim can seem to be an apologist for the very forms of power critiqued by Foucault; Dreyfus and Rabinow, for example, highlight Foucault's "inversion" of Durkheim's story of the triumph of science, individualism, and the objectivity of the social (Dreyfus and Rabinow 1983: 143). Durkheim's discussions of education, discipline and duty do trade on a broad evolutionary theme of the development of individualism and social differentiation (Gane 1992: 4), often characterised as triumphalist. But Durkheim's "genetic emphasis" (Vogt 1983: 192) bears comparison to Foucault's genealogical approach inasmuch as both try to articulate the specific and contingent origins of taken-for-granted universals, and do so on similar subject-matters. But let us first outline this evolutionary story.

Durkheim distinguished between primordial, undifferentiated groups (a theoretical limit case of the social), and organised societies (however simple) with some internal differentiation and some form of constituted authority.[2] The social appeared in a meaningful — that is, representable — sense only through differentiation and a consequent recognition of distinctions, from others and from nature. Such differentiation engendered a dialectic of particularity and totality constitutive of social life: for example, the particular identity of given social groupings in relation to the totality of all there is (humanity, all things associated with humans, and the world they inhabit). As a consequence of the process by which differentiated groups and then persons came to represent, remember and embody an idea of totality, Durkheim postulated that individuals ultimately came to see themselves both as particular and as partakers of a whole, embodying "souls" and thereby self-conscious and responsible moral subjects: representatives of the moral community which they, in turn, enact (Durkheim [1950a] 1957a: 161–162; Pearce 1989: 88–117). In *Professional Ethics and Civic Morals*, Durkheim claimed that property, initially collective[3] and landed, was first defined by its withdrawal from the common by particular groups; a process in which it came to be seen *as* property (and as sacred), and the group which held it as a *distinctive* group in relation to the gods symbolising the whole from which appropriation had taken place ([1950a] 1957a: 129–163). Property later became individualised *via* an evolutionary process in which particular members of such groups (for example, patriarchal heads of ancient Roman families) came to *represent* the group, and to hold its property *as* its representative. Some of this representative function eventually devolved to sons, by degrees to other men, and ultimately, we might say, to all accorded the definition human. From a patriarch as particular representative of the Roman family, Durkheim arrived ultimately at the individual as representative of humanity (ibid.: 165–173).

Relations between patriarchs and groups defined by their paternity would have been bound by a protocol in terms of which the patriarch, precisely as representative, would be treated in certain senses as sacred: his relations with other objects sacred to the group and with members of the group safeguarded by strict rules abjuring trespass and contamination. In societies marked by mechanical solidarity and strong kin organisation, one might also expect common rules of conduct accompanied by strict religious sanctions: in such instances, transgression of the prerogatives of a representative figure would take the form of "offences against the collective", and punishment, as Durkheim argued in "Two Laws of Penal Evolution", would tend to be harsh and vengeful, not only against offenders but also against their kin ([1901a (i)] 1992a: 34, 38–43). But with the development of individualism, contractual exchange and modern forms of citizenship, the intensity of punishment would lessen, the focus shifting from the bodies of offenders (or their kin) to deprivations of liberty and the inculcation of a sense of individual responsibility (ibid.: 32). Like Fustel de Coulanges, Durkheim linked these developments to a progressive defamilisation of the public realm (ibid.: 44; see also [1950a] 1957a: 115): as family life was restricted to the sphere of the "conjugal bond" and its products, governance, punishment and the regulation of property became less particularised and arbitrary. Crime came ultimately to be defined less as a trespass against the prerogatives of a ruler / father / representative than as a breaking of social bonds with others, now conceived of as equals (Durkheim [1901a (i)] 1992a: 38–43), and with oneself as a moral being. Punishment now aimed to restore a balance in social relations between equals, and to reconnect the offender to the "soul", the seat of individual moral agency.

However, the existence of hierarchical differentiation in all but the most "elementary" groups entailed sanctions to protect some members from trespass by others; sanctions exercised differently depending on the nature of the trespass and the social place of the offender. "Two Laws of Penal Evolution" distinguished "offences against the collective" from those "against persons", but went on to say that relative intensity of punishment could be an index not only of evolutionary differentiation or individualisation, but also of another factor, "absolutism". When sovereignty is not "counterbalanced" or constrained, is "hyper-centralised" or exercised "unilaterally", rulers can become, in a sense, super-human, freed from mitigating factors existing in juridical relations among equals, and punishment may thereby become "extreme" even in relatively modern societies (ibid.: 22–23, 30–31). Nonetheless, with the progressive dissolution of sovereignty based on the courtly apparatuses of family or estate, Durkheim held that the universalisation and objectification of society had become increasingly evident. Sovereignty now rested in the rule of law, expressed in and guaranteed by the conduct of individual citizens, and of individualised organs of social life, of which the state, a distinct, self-organised set of public bodies upholding the rights and prerogatives of individuals, is paramount. In committing a crime, one now trespasses against all and against oneself. For Durkheim, the social agency which would define and defend the moral attributes of "all" and "oneself" would be the state.

However, the existence of states as guarantors of individual rights was, Durkheim noted, insufficient to ensure either the emotional loyalty of individual citizens or moral cohesion in the spheres of production and distribution. Organisations mediating between state and individual were needed to exercise a pastoral role. Families were too turned in on themselves to provide more than elementary guidance to proper citizenship, and the loyalties of the Church were too an outmoded moral code and hierarchy. Nevertheless, the historical universality of the Church, as counter to the particular power of nobles and kings, provided a template for the new universal authority of national states and ultimately of international federations. But parish pastorates, guild corporations and professions did point to modern analogues which might again provide points of identification, forums for working out values specific to a given "branch of industry", and organisational structures through which mutual aid or social assistance might be provided. However, such "corporations" would not be free to provide two central functions of modern social life: criminal justice and education. In Durkheim's France, these were ultimately prerogatives of the national state, and sites of debates over the constitution of a national moral order. Beyond this historical contingency, modern education and criminal justice have to do with the formation and reformation of individuals; both, therefore, could be seen properly as the jurisdiction of the state in its role as guarantor of individual rights and defender of society as a whole. Thus, despite Durkheim's remarks about the "remoteness" of the state from individuals, its agencies would have intimate contact with individuals in two important areas of social life. Older guild models of apprenticeship and mutual aid could perhaps apply to some forms of professional socialisation, insurance and industrial training, or to adjudication mechanisms for specific industrial disputes. But ultimate control of citizenship training, the regulation and defence of the rights of individuals as citizens, and the regulation of property, would remain the jurisdiction of the state.

Durkheim's account of the evolution of modern sovereignty and authority can be both compared and contrasted to Foucault's thesis in *Discipline and Punish*. Foucault's description of punishment in the *ancien regime*, placing visible marks of power on the offender as retribution for trespass against the king's symbolic body, begs comparison to Durkheim's account of the penal consequences of absolutism. Both Foucault and Durkheim displayed an interest in the religious roots of secular phenomena (Alexander 1988b: 6): in Foucault's account, the King who exacts vengeance on Damiens does so as a sacred being in the Durkheimian sense (Hunt 1988: 32). In later "penitential" models of punishment by contrast, offenders were deprived of liberty as a first step to being induced to recover their "souls", to regain moral *self*-sovereignty. They thus came to be seen, not as exemplars of a particular "estate" but as individuals. Both Durkheim and Foucault, if in different ways, stressed this individualisation of modern punishment: the rise of "gentler" means of correction to restore offenders to themselves *via* pedagogical self-examination, thereby making them again fit for full citizenship. Foucault's account differs from Durkheim's less in that he described different things, but in that he saw the same events as part of a new articulation of power, rather than as a lessening of punitive severity. But even this insight is not entirely absent from Durkheim's account, if valued and reported differently.

4 Education and the soul

For Durkheim, as for many educational reformers from Pestalozzi onwards, education was a modernising project, intended to take children out of the limiting worlds of village and family (Durkheim [1925a] 1961a: 17–19, 146–148). But where Pestalozzi had emphasised practical training to integrate peasants into a modern, national capitalist agriculture, Durkheim stressed *moral* training for citizenship as part of the dissemination of a scientifically-grounded *morale laïque* appropriate to modern, secular society. Children were to be integrated into national social life through the intermediary of the school, the collective environment of which was to be a training ground for social duty, solidarity, moral autonomy and citizenship (ibid.: 1–14, 95–126, 230–231; Stock-Morton 1988: 125–153); in short, for the practical development of conscience.

Durkheim's treatment of educational practice in *Moral Education* resembles his discussion of the individualisation of punishment in that both refer to the constitution or reconstitution of moral individuals. Wilful or irregular personalities (children, criminals) would become responsible subjects by being made objects of pedagogical intervention: Durkheim claimed that children's "suggestibility" and "tendency to habit" made them susceptible to socialisation ([1925a] 1961a: 130–135). Yet children were best led to consciousness of themselves as citizens not by "senseless" rote instruction (ibid.: 183), but through exercises inducing them to act toward authority and each other in such a manner that they would come to think of themselves as responsible citizens and members of society. Similarly, noting that corporal punishment and "unruliness" tend to go together, Durkheim suggested that punishment be a pedagogical demonstration of the collective will (and not of the teacher's authority, except as representative of that will). He understood punishment, then, as a symbol, a "notation, a language" aimed at the conscience both of offenders and of witnesses. He also suggested the use of group self-policing in the classroom to encourage a moral consciousness (ibid.: 160, 166–167, 183, 244–246). Such examples make it clear that, despite different evaluations of such phenomena, both Durkheim and Foucault stressed the practices through which subjects of educational discipline, deprived of liberty to do what they want and objectified as targets of pedagogical technique, were none the less induced to engage in *conscious* self-recognition and *autonomous* self-regulation under the eye of authority. Both, in other words, described the practical formation of subjective identity as a process which *objectifies and re-subjectifies* those in the course of formation. Both noted that such a process had as its object the production not simply of dutiful yet autonomous individuals, but also of self-regulating, moral populations.

It is in his lectures on the historical development of French higher education that Durkheim's discussion of pedagogy acquires a most distinctively Foucaultian flavour. In *The Evolution of Educational Thought in France*, Durkheim defined his subject-matter neither as a history of educational philosophy, nor as a technical survey, nor as a simple linkage of the two. Instead, the term *pédagogie* would indicate what might be called practical philosophies of education, practices informed by particular definitions of the nature and place of education, educators and the educable. For Durkheim, neither the universals of educational theory nor applied teaching methods existed in their own right: they were animated by a third term, a sphere of action and speech in which institutional conflict, socioeconomic transformation and political innovation held sway. Formal educational philosophies, no less than practical techniques were effects — epiphenomena — of this third sphere of "practical theory", "an intermediary between art and science" (Collins 1977: xix; see also Lukes 1973: 11, n. 9). In short, Durkheim proposed to examine the specific social organisation of education; however, this is also a tale of social *dis*organisation, discontinuity, contestation and rupture. De-emphasising a protostructuralist classification of types or of stages of development, Durkheim explored the ragged world of actual historical transitions and irruptions. If the story told was still evolutionary, it was marked by a healthy respect for the contingencies by which the taken-for-granted world of modern pedagogy was constructed. Despite a continued emphasis on the discovery of invariant "laws" of social development and organisation, Durkheim's historico-sociological description, like Foucault's archaeology, also stressed specific forms of explanation, treating social developments *sui generis* and refusing to dive behind them to develop a story based on the eternal presence of taken-for-granted universals of human nature. *The Evolution of Educational Thought* displays a quasi-genealogical emphasis on the contingent, political and conflictual development of educational institutions, practices and philosophies (see Cherkaoui 1981).[4]

Durkheim's thesis in *The Evolution of Educational Thought* clearly parallels certain substantive themes in the latter volumes of Foucault's *History of Sexuality* series, *The Use of Pleasure*

(1985) and *The Care of the Self* (1986). The book is marked by a dramatic tension between the contingency of events in the history of modern education and the trends into which they coalesced over time. Significant among the latter was a turning-inward of the conditions of the moral life in Christianity, emphasising the moral status of individuals and individual intention (Tole 1993: 20). This led to a conception of education as productive of "a certain attitude of the soul... a certain *habitus* of our moral being" facilitating personal conversion. In contrast to classical forms of education in which different subjects were taught without co-ordination, education in Christendom became a socialising process, a focused exercise in the "production of Christians", with the unity of the pupil's personality as its integrating object: schooling as formation of the subject and mastery of the soul (Durkheim [1938a] 1977a: 28–30; Cherkaoui 1981). This process entailed an accentuation of personal relations between teacher and pupil such that the pupil was never left alone, and an individualisation of pupils such that learning became a process of inculcation dependent on individual effort and merit. These strategies led to individualised forms of competition and examination which in turn helped foster new institutional forms: the school as unified environment or "social community",[5] providing what Goffman might have called a total institutional setting for a totalising pedagogy of souls (see Giddens 1978: 77). In Christianity, truth was conceived of as a unity (implicit here is a hint at a genetic account of the development of Western rationalism), and this conception carried over into secular learning: to shape the mind as a whole, science itself needed to be conceived of as a whole (Durkheim [1938a] 1977a: 46).

Through such broad cultural transformations impelled by contingent political events,[6] an "encyclopedic" form of education developed which resisted parochial concerns in order to envelop the intelligence in its entirety (ibid.: 46, 81, 84). The outcome was modern scientific rationalism, which Durkheim claimed to be a cumulative universal of modern human experience while at the same time demonstrating the contingency of individual events constituting its specific history:

> [Science] represents, at each moment of its history, a kind of resume of human experience as this has been concentrated and accumulated year after year, from generation to generation. Its intellectual worth is consequently and quite naturally infinitely greater than that of individual minds operating on their own and without recourse to anything other than themselves. This explains why it is from science that we have everything to learn; in science, we find a kind of exemplary rationality which is the ideal model upon which our individual rationalities should seek to model themselves. Philosophers have often speculated that, beyond the bounds of human understanding, there is a kind of universal and impersonal understanding in which individual minds seek to participate by mystical means; well, this kind of understanding exists, and it exists not in any transcendent world but in this world itself. It exists in the world of science; or at least that is where it progressively realises itself; and it constitutes the ultimate source of logical vitality to which individual human rationality can attain. (ibid: 340–341)

Like Durkheim's, Foucault's later studies of the genesis of the modern self covered millennia instead of the mere century chronicled in *Discipline and Punish*. Foucault also took a genetic approach to the "philosophy of the subject" (Marshall 1990: 14), charting a process in which persons came to be taken as individual *totalities*, subjects of totalising regimes of confessional discipline and *self*-discipline, through an interiorisation which constituted them as an internalised *pair*: teacher-student, or confessor-penitent (e.g., Foucault 1986; Hoskin 1990). This is a history of the means by which human beings in Western culture have at once been made subjects, and objectified, by processes of classification and division (Ball 1990b: 3–4).

In *Discipline and Punish*, Foucault referred to the extension of the institutional practices of the penitentiary beyond prison walls, in the form of police surveillance, the classification and separation of populations, and incentives (provided by the new "psy" professions and their accompanying popular literatures) for individualised members of such populations to engage in disciplinary and confessional self-surveillance. As several commentators have noted (D. Jones 1990; Marshall 1990: 22–26; Hoskin 1990: 30–31), *Discipline and Punish* is as much about *educational* discipline as it is about correction. Durkheim's account of the development of modern educational institutions and practices begs, in an age of continuing education and retraining, to be developed in a similar manner. Is the generalisation of the "unified environment" of the school and the doctrine of self-improvement creating an "educational" society analogous to a carceral one? One might recall that the historical universalisation of education noted by Durkheim took institutional form at the primary level at the urging of those, following Smith and Bentham (D. Jones 1990) or Talleyrand (R. Jones 1990: 85), who saw the formation of the inhabitants of the "vast workshop" of the nation as too important to be left to private, parochial hands.

5   Two accounts of the modern subject

This now brings us to the question of how Durkheim's accounts of the evolution of the modern individual, and of the
institutional forms surrounding that development, might help
shed light on what Foucault, Donzelot and others term the development of "governmentality" or of "police" since the
eighteenth century (Foucault 1988b, 1991; Donzelot, 1991,
1993; Gane and Johnson 1993b; Hoskin 1990; Miller and Rose
1993; Pasquino 1991, 1993; Procacci 1991). Donzelot's own
response is to treat Durkheimian sociology as an example of the
governmentalist discourse accompanying that "positive" transformation and expansion of power Foucault termed biopolitics:
the identification of populations, families and individuals as
sites of surveillance and normalising intervention by states,
philanthropic agencies, professionals and the like. Donzelot
(1991: 34, 41, 172–3) calls Durkheim's emphasis on solidarity
(which he links to Léon Bourgeois' *solidarisme*) a rationale for
state intervention, beyond juridical, legal and economic matters,
into the "social bond" itself. Such expanded intervention was
also promoted by a school within the late nineteenth-century
enterprise of social economy which sought to modify or mitigate
relations between labour and capital, and to "concretise the
invisible bond between men of which the state is the visible
expression", *via* the "insurance technique" (Donzelot 1993:
109–112). Hacking includes Durkheim in his account of the
"avalanche of numbers" that accompanied the rise of governmentality: an explosion of statistics-gathering in the context of
efforts by Quételet, Galton and others to define the "normal" in
human capacities and associations (Hacking 1991: 183, 187–9).
While Durkheim attempted a sophisticated sociological version
of the normal-pathological distinction, and while his use of
statistics was in part an applied critique of the slapdash use of

numbers by contemporaries, his attempt is solidly situated in a larger discursive context.

Durkheim's uncritical approbation of the individualisation of punishment and the development of education as a socialising enterprise could easily be taken as evidence of a close fit between his agenda and the normalising thrust of modern state and professional intervention into social life, as Foucault himself implies. An ensemble of disciplinary practices begging to be analysed in their specificity (see Gane and Johnson 1993b: 7), instead become part of a larger "story" — of progressive individualism, of the rise of the state as a guarantor of individual rights and the social bond, of national educational reform: all developments supposedly "immanent" in the history of modernity (e.g., Durkheim [1938a] 1977a: 46). Durkheim's adherence to the *morale laïque* ideal, and his own political connections strengthen this case, as do his characterisation of discipline as a key property of society and his emphasis on the coexistence of individual autonomy and communal welfare as moral requirements of modern societies, fostered *via* the promotion of an affective loyalty to a scientifically-defensible moral order. (Tole 1993: 6–7, 22; Durkheim [1924a] 1974a: 35–62). Even his emphasis on the disengagement of modern pedagogy and morality from religious, ethnic and geographical particularity (Schoenfeld and Meštrovic 1991: 89) can be read as a variant of a broad, urban-centred discourse of modernisation in terms of which rural, precapitalist and non-"productive" populations (for example, the recalcitrant Irish described by Procacci 1991: 155, 158–62) were denigrated as indolent and backward, and subjected to normalising forms of economic, juridical and social intervention.

But despite such parallels, Durkheimian sociology did not prove directly useful to agencies involved in normalising interventions into social life. If, as Richman (1995: 59) notes,

Durkheim had links to solidarist circles in *fin de siècle* syndicalism and socialism, his was an anomalous and critical relation. As a fellow-traveller on the governmentalist itinerary, Durkheim was not particularly effective on the ground, in part due to the general, abstract nature of his work: even his educational prescriptions did not make for practical classroom manuals. But there is another reason for the limited practical use made of Durkheim in social intervention, one that partly explains its characterisation as "abstract", for the tag is, to a degree, political. Durkheim's sociology is resolutely *sociological*, resisting reduction to the level of individual psychology, and suspending a taken-for-granted acceptance of the category of the individual subject as an entry point for social analysis or intervention. Durkheim approved of Comte's assertion that "the old anthropocentric conception of man was finished once the law of universal gravitation had been discovered" (Durkheim [1938a] 1977a: 339), and himself sought to depart from an "ontology of the self", as did Foucault (Gane and Johnson 1993b: 6–7). He treated both individuality and subjectivity as social phenomena and effects of social evolution, not merely in the sense that individuals were "influenced" by the social, but in that they *had meaning as categories* only in given sociocultural contexts.[7] This view of individuals and persons bears comparison to Foucault's "history of the problematisations of subjectivity" (Pasquino 1993: 41–42), and his assertion that the individual subject is not an "elementary nucleus" of social life but an effect of power, gestures and discourses (Taylor 1985: 294).

Conversely, "psy" disciplines or agencies engaged in the normalisation of individuals and populations rely on a concept of the individual subject which they *must* assume and cannot suspend: a subject with needs, propensities, desires, points of influence and developmental stages to be obsessively enumerated, classified and analysed. This subject's relation to the social is *external*: to society hypostasised as a set of "influences" (peer groups, cultures of poverty, gangs, families, police, *etc.*) *acting on* it. It is an effect of social intervention: the constructed site of its practice and its discourse object. If Durkheim treated individual subjectivity as a given of modern social life, and as a site of intervention, he defined it precisely in terms of its social matrix and the agencies it confronts, rejecting an hypostasised subject-object dualism in both his epistemology and his substantive work (Meštrovic 1988: 40–53). In interrogating the status of the individual as subject (the development of the "soul"), he necessarily addressed the status of objects and contexts, and *vice versa. The subject and the objective social world are formed in relation to each other, and the vehicles of that correlative formation are collective representations.* This stance allowed Durkheim to perceive "social formations that defy standard sociological categorisation", and to develop a new *topique* "located between the sociological and the political" (Richman 1995: 62), but in consequence, a Durkheimian take on social intervention could not suspend the question of the *social status* of that intervention: a suspension that social work has often successfully, if never perfectly, maintained.

None the less, a Durkheimian theory of moral education or of penal evolution does not constitute an analytics of power in a Foucaultian sense. If Durkheim did not mean to erect an evolutionary teleology, he did argue that laws of social development, indeed any objectively-ascertainable laws of social life, really exist (inasmuch as they are ascertainable), and thus are not radically contingent.[8] Contingency would characterise variations: premodern survivals persisting as pathologies in modern life; for example, inheritance, and perhaps absolutism.[9] Foucault, conversely, emphasised precisely the contingent and particular development of social technologies of power, as in the confessional models of self-examination and self-discipline encouraged by social work, psychiatry and so on. The power implicit in these practices is not simply the property of agents (whether professionals, the state, a class, etc.); agents themselves are instituted in the very statements and practices through which objects (of normalising policies, surveillance, interrogation and moral exhortation) come into being. This is not to say that no broad patterns appear in Foucault's narrative, but that they do not employ a standard cast. Foucault traced the development of a model of human being organised in terms of an "empirico-transcendental doublet": humanity as subjective author of its fate, and as of a gaze which opens its anatomy and minutely records its behaviour. This duality is held together by an economy of truth: an anatomo-politics of the individual body, and a management of categorised populations that Foucault termed biopower, operating through exhaustive information-gathering and the institution of measures by which individuals are policed and induced to become self-policing. In this order, questions of political sovereignty take new forms (the rule of citizens and their representatives, the sovereign *self*-rule of the responsible citizen), but Foucault drove a wedge between sovereignty and power to explore the development of *governmentality*: a myriad of ways in which social agencies, not all directly related to the state, encouraged the development of a regulated and self-regulating society and of individuals as clients.

6   Conclusions

Whether the various parallels between Durkheim and Foucault could be called linkages would make for an interesting exercise in intellectual history. One avenue of research would be to explore the likelihood of direct or mediated Durkheimian influences on Foucault; another would be to investigate the extent to which Lévi-Strauss, Althusser, Foucault and others all participated in (or, were constituted as authors in terms of) discursive formations and horizons of expectation still resonant with those articulating the Durkheimian project. But neither possibility merits study if the parallels on which they are based are of no interest in their own right. Does a comparison with Durkheim illuminate our understanding of Foucault, or vice versa?

As has been suggested, Durkheim can be read through a Foucaultian lens as an advocate of the sort of modernising governmentality Foucault sought to expose: Durkheim's proposals for moral education can be read as a social technology for the production of self-governing subjects, and his attempt to establish a scientific basis for social policy and practice can be interpreted as part of a process by which the social was invented as a discourse-object and as a terrain of normalising intervention. But as we have noted, Durkheim is not the best example of this process. The "social" discourse developed in philanthropic agencies, social work, educational institutions and moral uplift groups emphasised social determinations affecting the behaviour and predilections of *individuals*. Durkheim's insistent emphasis on the methodological and practical implications of the existence of the social *sui generis* was forgotten in a rush to treat the social merely as a set of determinations affecting individual behaviour.

Another reading of Durkheim might be to force suggestions in his sociology beyond his own limits; for example, extending his analysis of representation in a manner akin to his and Mauss's linkage of failed reciprocity to violence or exploitation. In the process of differentiation constitutive of a dialectic of particularity and totality, society becomes objectified, identifiable through emblematic objects, rites, etc. With these externalised entities, and persons associated with them, exchange relations, including sacrificial exchange and even ritual violence, may be set up. What if particular individuals or groups with a representative function in social life — symbolising or embodying the social — came to act in anomic ways no longer reflective of the organic integrity of social life and no longer recognisant of restraint or obligation? More to the point, what if the very discourse of social itself became anomic such that the category "society" ceased to represent the collective life of most people and became instead an abstraction (Sayer 1991) marking external determinations placed on "individuals" who maintain externalised relations to "it"? (Consider the journalistic use of the noun, "society", as the subject of phrases like, "Society causes us to", "or Society dictates that we...".) What if we were to analyse current representations of the social as projections defined by the agendas of agencies charged not with returning an anomic *society* to its normal functioning, but with returning deviant or "irresponsible" *individuals* to a norm of self-monitoring and self-interrogating responsibility on behalf of a normalising authority charged with their management?

In such possibilities might lie the beginning of a fertile Durkheim-Foucault dialogue concerning unequal (violent, enslaving) forms of exchange and skewed representation evident when "individual" and "social" are set in external relation to each other. But possibilities can be interpreted differently. A Durkheimian might term the disciplinary phenomena illuminated by Foucault pathological: a perversion of liberal individualism and communitarianism. But from a genealogical standpoint, they would appear not as pathologies or departures from a norm, but precisely *as the normalising machinery by which modern individualism constructs its truth*: the dark side of utopian dreams of citizenship, community and individual autonomy. Here, arguably, lies a basic split between Durkheim and Foucault, but one with an interesting history. A late attempt to resurrect a distinctively Durkheimian project marked the work of *the Collège de Sociologie*, founded in 1937 by Michel Leiris, Roger Caillois and Georges Bataille (Richman 1995; Bataille, 1988) to develop a "sacred sociology" with a Durkheimian methodology and informed by the anthropology of Mauss. The project collapsed in disagreement, and Bataille's subsequent literary career owed more to Nietzsche than to Durkheim. However, it can be argued that Bataille played Nietzsche to the ghost of Durkheimian sociologism. The god whose death he announced was Durkheimian social ontology: the idea of society-as-God and a normative distinction between normalcy and pathology. Given Bataille's importance to Foucault's intellectual trajectory, one might suggest that Foucault's own Nietzschean posture be understood in light of traditions of French historiography and anthropology linked to Durkheim and Mauss, and before them, Saint-Simon, Comte and Fustel de Coulanges.

In "A Preface to Transgression" (1977b), Foucault wrote that limit and transgression, after the death of God, no longer have a transcendent meaning: the transgressive act illuminates the limit at the moment it is undertaken. One is tempted to read this as an atheist (in)version of a sociologistic faith expressed by Durkheim in *The Rules of Sociological Method*: social facts may be known by their external constraint — a force Durkheim described as experienced *precisely at the moment* at which a social norm is transgressed. The Durkheimian concept of anomie rests on a definition of the social (and of individual subjects) in terms of limits set by categories and classifications. As long as the social can be said to exist meaningfully, these limits define and place subjects in a meaningful world. With its death, subjectivity and political agency would become radically contingent, their meaning illuminated in the instant of their deployment, rather than bathed in the growing light of an evolutionary dawn.

NOTES

1. I wish to thank David Brown for his valuable suggestions concerning the following sections. Responsibility for their implementation, and for any errors therein, remains mine.

2. For Durkheim, modern societies derive from "elementary" differentiated social forms, not primordial "hordes". Further, the family is itself an effect of an organised social context, not the ancestor of all subsequent social authority; see Durkheim [1950a] 1957a: 45–47.

3. Durkheim's genetic account of property owed much to Fustel de Coulanges (1956: 60–84). The latter became increasingly sceptical of the idea that property was originally communal (Fustel de Coulanges 1927), and opposed romanticised ideas of "primitive communism". Durkheim's use of the term "collective" is, however, distinct from such ideas.

4. Durkheim's discussion of educational practice in the classical era is indebted to Fustel: the whole work is marked by an approach to historical description of which Durkheim called Fustel a master (Halbwachs 1977: xiii). As an agenda for further study, one might suggest that Durkheim's genetic account of the origins of modern categories of thought and action (and of modern institutions), and Foucault's genealogies, might be linked through the role of Fustel in the development of French historiography. Foucault stressed the importance of Nietzsche to his work; one might ask what horizons of expectation made Nietzsche attractive to him.

5. Durkheim's discussion of the institution of the convict ([1938a] 1977a: 28) calls out for a Foucaultian etymological genealogy.

6. Another general theme of the study was the gradual, conflictual disengagement of higher education from local or religious ties, to emerge as a national and international phenomenon. Medieval corporations of teachers in Paris gained solidarity and identity opposing groups blocking their rise to influence; battling local ecclesiastical interests *via* a "strange alliance" with the papacy against its own hierarchy. Centuries later, Jesuit educational reforms responded to the Reformation in a manner that weakened the

hegemony of the University, a set of political contingencies which long after marked the Jesuit impact on modern secondary education (Durkheim [1938a] 1977a: 75–87, 227–264).

7. In discussing the dualism of human nature, Durkheim ([1914a] 1960c) rejected traditional individual/society oppositions to claim that individual interests, while rooted in bodily particularity, are only definable as *self*-interest in a social context. As conscious, social subjects, individuals, are not simply "constrained" by the social but liberated and protected from "blind, unthinking physical forces" by submission to it (Durkheim [1924a] 1974a: 72). Mauss, too (1985: 49), insisted that individual personhood, like other categories of modern life, originated in and was defined by specific social contexts, however "essential" it might appear to those living in a "culture of the personal".

8. It is worth noting Durkheim's comments on the place of grammar in medieval pedagogy (Durkheim [1938a] 1977a: 60–73). Debates over the ontology of grammatical constructions constituted early attempts to "confront faith with reason". Realists defended the real existence of grammatical "kinds", attributes or genera; for example, the "soul" as a really existing generic principle individualised in personal form. Durkheim traced modern philosophical realism back to a specific concatenation of pedagogical techniques, religious beliefs and ecclesiastical interests. By the same token, his own "realist" tendencies did not reflect an abstract epistemology: for Durkheim, categories, including scientific categories, are "real" inasmuch as they are *social facts*, that is, collective representations (Durkheim [1912a] 1915d: 238–239, 477–496). A similar point could be made about Foucault's conception of discourse.

9. Durkheim argued that modern contracts were not simply exercises in self-interest, but social bonds necessitating a mutual recognition of shared values and meanings articulating exchange, and constituting a shared humanity. Forced or unjust contracts based on inheritance, like unequal gift exchange (Mauss), deny the commonality of the contracting parties, setting one up in a position to deny the autonomy and humanity of the other. The consequence, as Mauss (1990) put it, is war or slavery. In unequal contracts between capital and labour, outcomes include businesses which operate as if

they owe society nothing, and class conflict. (It is noteworthy that while Mauss eschewed Durkheimian social ontology for more specific empirical studies, his essay on the gift is organised in terms of a Durkheimian ontological thematics.) Though Durkheim did not develop an analysis of absolutism as a pathology, it could similarly be argued that absolutist states cease to represent the social order and instead take on an anomic will of their own over against society, acting, to paraphrase Brecht, as if "the people" constitute mere objects to be revised or cancelled: targets of modification, persuasion, surveillance and exploitation, or of power/knowledge in the Foucaultian sense. There is much here that begs further analysis; for example, the idea that social welfare might become an exchange enslaving those defined by it as "dependent" — an exchange of benefits for the right to extract information and to regulate. But Durkheim did not explore these possibilities in any depth.

REFERENCES

References to Durkheim follow the system initiated by Lukes: see Foreword

Alexander, J. C., ed. 1988a. *Durkheimian Sociology: Cultural Studies.* Cambridge: CUP.

Alexander, J. C. 1988b. "Introduction: Durkheimian sociology and cultural studies today", in Alexander 1988a.

Althusser, L. 1969. *For Marx.* Harmondsworth: Allen Lane.

Ball, S. J., ed. 1990a. *Foucault and Education: Disciplines and Knowledge.* London: Routledge.

Ball, S. J. 1990b. "Introducing Monsieur Foucault", in Ball 1990a.

Bataille, G. 1988. "The College of Sociology", in D. Hollier, ed., *The College of Sociology (1937–39).* Minneapolis: University of Minnesota Press.

Besnard, P., ed. 1983a. *The Sociological Domain: The Durkheimians and the Founding of French Sociology.* Cambridge: CUP.

Besnard, P. 1983b. "The Année sociologique team", in Besnard 1983a.

Burchell, G., C. Gordon and P. Miller (eds.) 1991. *The Foucault Effect: Studies in Governmentality.* Chicago: University of Chicago Press.

Cherkaoui, M. 1981. "Two Theories of Change in Educational Systems: Bernstein and Durkheim", in C. C. Lemert, ed., *French Sociology: Rupture and Renewal Since 1968*. New York: Columbia University Press.

Collins, P. 1977. "Translator's Introduction", in Durkheim [1938a] 1977a.

Craig, J. E. 1983. "Sociology and related disciplines between the wars: Maurice Halbwachs and the imperialism of the Durkheimians", in Besnard 1983a.

Donzelot, J. 1991. "The mobilization of society", in Burchell, Gordon and Miller 1991.

Donzelot, J. 1993. "The Promotion of the Social", in Gane and Johnson 1993a.

Dreyfus, H. L. and P. Rabinow. 1983. *Michel Foucault: Beyond Structuralism and Hermeneutics*, 2nd ed. Chicago: University of Chicago Press.

Durkheim, E. [1893b] 1984a. *The Division of Labour in Society*. London: Macmillan.

Durkheim, E. [1900b] 1973a. "Sociology in France in the Nineteenth Century", in R. Bellah, ed., *Emile Durkheim on Morality and Society*. Chicago: University of Chicago Press.

Durkheim, E. [1901a (i)] 1992a."Two Laws of Penal Evolution", in M. Gane, ed., *The Radical Sociology of Durkheim and Mauss*. London: Routledge.

Durkheim, E. [1912a] 1915d. *The Elementary Forms of the Religious Life: A Study in Religious Sociology*. London: George Allen and Unwin.

Durkheim, E. [1914a] 1960c. "The Dualism of Human Nature", in K. Wolff, ed., *Emile Durkheim, 1858–1917*. Columbus: Ohio State University Press.

Durkheim, E. [1924a] 1974a. *Sociology and Philosophy*. New York: Free Press.

Durkheim, E. [1925a] 1961a. *Moral Education*. New York: Free Press.

Durkheim, E. [1938a] 1977a. *The Evolution of Educational Thought*. London: Routledge & Kegan Paul.

Durkheim, E. [1950a] 1957a. *Professional Ethics and Civic Morals*. London: Routledge & Kegan Paul.

Durkheim, E. and M. Mauss. [1903a (i)] 1963b. *Primitive Classification*. Chicago: University of Chicago Press.

Foucault, M. 1972. *The Archaeology of Knowledge*. London: Tavistock.

Foucault, M. 1977a. *Discipline and Punish*. New York: Tavistock.

Foucault, M. 1977b. "A Preface to Trangression", in D. F. Bouchard, ed., *Language, Counter-Memory, Practice*. Ithaca: Cornell University Press.

Foucault, M. 1977c. "Nietzsche, Genealogy, History", in D.F. Bouchard, ed., *Language, Counter-Memory, Practice*. Ithaca: Cornell University Press.

Foucault, M. 1978. *The History of Sexuality, vol. 1: An Introduction*. New York: Pantheon.

Foucault, M. 1985. *The History of Sexuality, vol. 2, The Use of Pleasure*. New York: Pantheon.

Foucault, M. 1986. *The History of Sexuality, vol. 3, The Care of the Self*. New York: Pantheon.

Foucault, M. 1988a. "Technologies of the Self", in Martin, Gutman and Hutton 1988.

Foucault, M. 1988b. "The Political Technology of Individuals", in Martin, Gutman and Hutton 1988.

Foucault, M. 1991. "Governmentality", in Burchell, Gordon and Miller 1991.

Foucault, M. 1993. "Kant on Enlightenment and revolution", in Gane and Johnson 1993a.

Fustel de Coulanges, N. D. 1927. *The Origin of Property in Land*. London: George Allen and Unwin.

Fustel de Coulanges, N. D. 1956. *The Ancient City: a Study on the Religion, Laws and Institutions of Greece and Rome*. New York: Doubleday Anchor Books.

Gane, M. 1988. *On Durkheim's Rules of Sociological Method*. London: Routledge.

Gane, M. 1992. "Introduction: Emile Durkheim, Marcel Mauss and the Sociological Project", in M. Gane, ed., *The Radical Sociology of Durkheim and Mauss*. London: Routledge.

Gane, M. and T. Johnson, eds. 1993a. *Foucault's New Domains*. London: Routledge.

Gane, M. and T. Johnson. 1993b. "Introduction: the Project of Michel Foucault", in Gane and Johnson 1993a.

Geiger, R. 1983. "Durkheimian Sociology under attack: the controversy over sociology in the Ecole Normale Primaires", in Besnard 1983a.

Giddens, A. 1978. *Durkheim: His Life, Work, Writings and Ideas.* Hassocks, Sussex: The Harvester Press.

Gordon, C. 1993. "Question, ethos, event: Foucault on Kant and Enlightenment", in Gane and Johnson 1993a.

Gutting, G. 1989. *Michel Foucault's Archaeology of Scientific Reason.* Cambridge: CUP.

Hacking, I. 1991. "How Should We Do the History of Statistics?", in Burchell, Gordon and Miller 1991.

Halbwachs, M. 1977. "Introduction to the French Edition of 1938", in Durkheim [1938a] 1977a.

Hoskin, K. 1990. "Foucault under examination: the crypto-educationalist unmasked", in Ball 1990a.

Hunt, L. 1988. "The Sacred and the French Revolution", in Alexander 1988a.

Jones, D. 1990. "The genealogy of the urban schoolteacher", in Ball 1990a.

Jones, R. 1990. "Educational practices and scientific knowledge: a genealogical reinterpretation of the emergence of physiology in post-Revolutionary France", in Ball 1990a.

Jones, R. A. and D. A. Kibbee. 1993. "Ambivalent Cartesians: Durkheim, Montesquieu and Method", *American Journal of Sociology*, 100 (1): 1–39.

Karady, V. 1981. "The Prehistory of Present-day French Sociology (1917–57)", in C. C. Lemert, ed., *French Sociology: Rupture and Renewal Since 1968.* New York: Columbia University Press.

Karady, V. 1983. "The Durkheimians in Academe: a reconsideration", in Besnard 1983a.

Lukes, S. 1973. *Emile Durkheim, His Life and Work: A Historical and Critical Study.* London: Allen Lane.

Lukes, S. and A. Scull. 1984. "Introduction", in S. Lukes and A. Scull, eds., *Durkheim and the Law.* Oxford: Blackwell.

Marshall, J. D. 1990. "Foucault and educational research", in Ball 1990a.

Martin, L. H., H. Gutman and P. H. Hutton, eds. 1988. *Technologies of the Self: a seminar with Michel Foucault.* Amherst, Massachusetts: University of Massachusetts Press.

Martin, R. 1988. "Truth, Power, Self: an interview with Michel Foucault", in Martin, Gutman and Hutton 1988.

Mauss, M. 1985. "A category of the human mind: the notion of person; the notion of self", in M. Carruthers, S. Collins and S. Lukes, eds.,

The Category of the Person: Anthropology, Philosophy, History. Cambridge: CUP.

Mauss, M. 1990. *The Gift*. New York: Norton.

Meštrovic, S. J. 1988. *Emile Durkheim and the Reformation of Sociology*. Totowa, N. J.: Rowman and Littlefield.

Miller, P. and N. Rose. 1993. "Governing Economic Life", in Gane and Johnson 1993a.

O'Neill, J. 1986. "The Disciplinary Society: from Weber to Foucault", *British Journal of Sociology* 37: 42–60.

Pasquino, P. 1991. "Theatrum politicum: The genealogy of capital — police and the state of prosperity", in Burchell, Gordon and Miller 1991.

Pasquino, P. 1993. "Michel Foucault (1926–84): The Will to Knowledge", in Gane and Johnson 1993a.

Patton, P. 1979. "Of Power and Prisons", in M. Morris and P. Patton, eds., *Michel Foucault: Power, Truth, Strategy*. Sydney: Feral Press.

Pearce, F. 1989. *The Radical Durkheim*. London: Unwin Hyman.

Procacci, G. 1991. "Social economy and the government of poverty", in Burchell, Gordon and Miller 1991.

Richman, M. 1982. *Reading Georges Bataille: Beyond the Gift*. Baltimore, Maryland: Johns Hopkins University Press.

Richman, M. 1995. "The Sacred Group: A Durkheimian perspective on the Collège de sociologie", in C. B. Gill, ed., *Bataille: Writing the Sacred*. London: Routledge.

Sayer, D. 1991. *Capitalism and Modernity*. New York: Routledge.

Schoenfeld, E. and S. G. Meštrovic. 1991. "From the Sacred Collectivity to the Sacred Individual: The Misunderstood Durkheimian Legacy", *Sociological Focus*, 24 (2).

Stock-Morton, P. 1988. *Moral Education for a Secular Society: The Development of Morale Laïque in Nineteenth-Century France*. Albany: State University of New York Press.

Taylor, C. 1985. "The Person", in M. Carruthers, S. Collins and S. Lukes, eds., *The Category of the Person: Anthropology, Philosophy, History*. Cambridge: CUP.

Tole, L.-A. 1993. "Durkheim on Religion and Moral Community in Modernity", *Sociological Inquiry*, 63 (1).

Vogt, W. P. 1983. "Obligation and right: the Durkheimians and the sociology of law", in Besnard 1983a.

Wernick, A. 1984. "Structuralism and the Dislocation of the French Rationalist Project", in J. Fekete, ed., *The Structural Allegory: Re-*

constructive Encounters with the New French Thought. Minneapolis: University of Minnesota Press.

Weisz, G. 1983. "The republican ideology and the social sciences; the Durkheimians and the history of social economy at the Sorbonne", in Besnard 1983a.

CONTRIBUTORS

Mark S. Cladis, author of *A Communitarian Defense of Liberalism: Emile Durkheim and Contemporary Social Theory* (Stanford University Press, 1992), is Associate Professor and Chair at Vassar College. After receiving his doctorate from Princeton University, where he studied philosophy and social theory as they relate to the field of religious studies, he taught at the University of North Carolina and at Stanford University. His publications and teaching are concerned with the history of Western political, social and religious thought, especially the religious nature and origins of liberal, democratic society. His current research project, *Politics of the Heart: Rousseau, Religion, and the Relation between the Public and Private Life*, is due to appear in 1999.

David Garland held a fellowship at Princeton University in 1984-85, taught at the University of California, Berkeley in 1988, went on to become Professor of Criminology at the University of Edinburgh, and is now Professor at New York University. He is author of many articles on criminology, penal theory and the sociology of law, as well as of *Punishment and Modern Society* (Oxford: Clarendon Press, 1990), a study and critique of the perspectives on law, society and punishment of Durkheim, Weber, Foucault and the Marxist tradition.

Werner Gephart, author of *Strafe und Verbrechen: die Theorie Emile Durkheims* (Opladen: Leske & Budrich, 1990) has been Professor of Sociology at the University of Bonn since 1992. He was Alfred Grosser Guest Professor at the Institut d'Etudes Politiques in Paris. His main interests are in the sociology of law, sociological theory, symbolism, culture and religion. His current projects include editing a critical edition of Max Weber's sociology of law.

W.S.F. Pickering, is a founder and the general secretary of the British Centre for Durkheimian Studies, Oxford. He has been active in organising its programme of seminars and international conferences, and in initiating and editing publications linked with it. These include *Debating Durkheim* (London: Routledge, 1994), *On Durkheim's Elementary Forms of Religious Life* (London: Routledge, 1998), *Durkheim and Modern Education* (London: Routledge, 1998), and, since 1995, a new series of the journal, *Durkheimian Studies / Etudes Durkheimiennes*. He is author, amongst other works, of *Durkheim's Sociology of Religion* (London: Routledge & Kegan Paul, 1984). His current projects include editing a collection on the key Durkheimian idea of "collective representations".

William Ramp is Assistant Professor of Sociology at the University of Lethbridge, Alberta, Canada. His doctoral thesis was on Talcott Parsons and the Parsonian interpretation of Durkheim. His articles include "Effervescence, differentiation and representation in *The Elementary Forms*", in N. J. Allen, W. S. F. Pickering and W. Watts Miller, eds., *On Durkheim's* Elementary Forms of Religious Life (London: Routledge, 1998), as well as his contribution to the present collection. His interests relate to sociological theories of identity and subjectivity as applied to religion and social movements.

BIBLIOGRAPHY

References to Durkheim follow the system initiated by Lukes: see Foreword

Alexander, J. C., ed. 1988a. *Durkheimian Sociology: Cultural Studies.* Cambridge: CUP.

Alexander, J. C. 1988b. "Introduction: Durkheimian sociology and cultural studies today", in Alexander 1988a.

Althusser, L. 1969. *For Marx.* Harmondsworth: Allen Lane.

Ariès, P. 1960. *L'Enfant et la familiale sous l'ancien règime.* Paris: Editions du Seuil.
(1962. *Centuries of Childhood*, trans. R. Baldwick. London: Jonathan Cape).

Ball, S. J., ed. 1990a. *Foucault and Education: Disciplines and Knowledge.* London: Routledge.

Ball, S. J. 1990b. "Introducing Monsieur Foucault", in Ball 1990a.

Bartlett, R. 1986. *Trial by Fire and Water.* Oxford: OUP.

Bataille, G. 1988. "The College of Sociology", trans. B. Wing, in D. Hollier, ed., *The College of Sociology (1937-39).* Minneapolis: University of Minnesota Press.

Besnard, P., ed. 1983a. *The Sociological Domain: The Durkheimians and the Founding of French Sociology.* Cambridge: CUP.

Besnard, P. 1983b. "The Année sociologique team", in Besnard 1983a.

Burchell, G., C. Gordon and P. Miller, eds. 1991. *The Foucault Effect: Studies in Governmentality.* Chicago: University of Chicago Press.

Cherkaoui, M. 1981. "Two Theories of Change in Educational Systems: Bernstein and Durkheim", in C. C. Lemert, ed., *French Sociology: Rupture and Renewal Since 1968.* New York: Columbia University Press.

Collins, P. 1977. "Translator's Introduction", in Durkheim [1938a] 1977a.

Craig, J. E. 1983. "Sociology and related disciplines between the wars: Maurice Halbwachs and the imperialism of the Durkheimians", in Besnard 1983a.

Dahrendorf, R. 1985. *Law and Order.* London: Stevens.

Donzelot, J. 1991. "The mobilization of society", in Burchell, Gordon and Miller 1991.

Donzelot, J. 1993. "The Promotion of the Social", in Gane and Johnson 1993a.

Dreyfus, H. L. and P. Rabinow. 1983. *Michel Foucault: Beyond Structuralism and Hermeneutics*, 2nd ed. Chicago: University of Chicago Press.

Durkheim, E. [1888a] 1970a. "Cours de science sociale. Leçon d'ouverture", in *La science sociale et l'action*, edited with introduction by J-C. Filloux. Paris: PUF.

Durkheim, E. [1893b] 1902b. *De la division du travail social*, 2nd edition. Paris: Alcan.

(1933b. *The Division of Labour in Society*, trans. G. Simpson. New York: Macmillan).

(1984a. *The Division of Labour in Society*, trans. W. D. Halls. London: Macmillan).

Durkheim, E. [1898a (iii) (13)] 1969c. Review of Mauss, *La Religion et les origines du droit pénal*, in *Journal sociologique*, with introduction and notes by J. Duvignaud. Paris: PUF.

Durkheim, E. [1900b] 1973a. "Sociology in France in the Nineteenth Century", trans. M. Traugott, in R. Bellah, ed., *Emile Durkheim on Morality and Society*. Chicago: University of Chicago Press.

Durkheim, E. 1901a (i). "Deux Lois de l'évolution pénale", *Année sociologique*, IV: 65-95.

(1969e. "Two Laws of Penal Evolution", trans. W. Jeffrey Jr., *University of Cincinnati Law Review*, 38: 32-60).

(1973b. "Two Laws of Penal Evolution", trans. T. Jones and A. Scull, in S. Lukes and A. Scull, eds., *Durkheim and the Law*. London: M. Robertson).

(1992a. ibid., in M. Gane, ed., *The Radical Sociology of Durkheim and Mauss*. London: Routledge).

Durkheim, E. [1901c] 1973. *Les règles de la méthode sociologique*, 18th edition. Paris: PUF.

Durkheim, E. [1906b] 1974a. "The Determination of Moral Facts", with replies to objections, in Durkheim [1924a] 1974a.

Durkheim, E. [1907d] 1975b. "Contribution à un débat de l'Union pour la vérité. Sur la réforme des institutions judiciares: l'enseignement du droit", in E. Durkheim, *Textes*, vol.1, ed., V. Karady. Paris: Editions de Minuit.

Durkheim, E. [1912a] 1915d. *The Elementary Forms of the Religious Life: A Study in Religious Sociology*, trans. J. W. Swain. London: George Allen and Unwin.

Durkheim, E. [1914a] 1960c. "The Dualism of Human Nature", trans. C. Blend, in K. Wolff, ed., *Emile Durkheim, 1858-1917*. Columbus: Ohio State University Press.

Durkheim, E. 1919a. "La 'Pédagogie' de Rousseau", *Revue de métaphysique et de morale*, XXVI: 153-180.

(1979a. "Rousseau on Educational Theory", trans. H. L. Sutcliffe, in W. S. F. Pickering, ed., *Durkheim: Essays on Morals and Education*. London: Routledge & Kegan Paul).

Durkheim, E. [1922a] 1956a. *Education and Sociology*, trans. S. D. Fox. Glencoe: Free Press.

Durkheim, E. [1924a] 1974a. *Sociology and Philosophy*, trans. D. F. Pocock. New York: Free Press.

Durkheim, E. 1925a. *L'Education morale*, introduction by Paul Fauconnet. Paris: Alcan.

(1961a. *Moral Education*, trans. E. K. Wilson and H. Schnurer. New York: Free Press).

Durkheim, E. [1938a] 1977a. *The Evolution of Educational Thought*, trans. P. Collins. London: Routledge & Kegan Paul.

Durkheim, E. [1950a] 1969g. *Leçons de sociologie: physique des mœurs et du droit*, 2nd edition. Paris: PUF.

(1957a. *Professional Ethics and Civic Morals*, trans. C. Brookfield. London: Routledge & Kegan Paul).

Durkheim, E. and M. Mauss. [1903a (i)] 1963b. *Primitive Classification*, translated and edited by R. Needham. Chicago: University of Chicago Press.

Fauconnet, P. 1920. *La responsabilité*. Paris: Alcan.

Foucault, M. 1972. *The Archaeology of Knowledge*, trans. A. M. Sheridan Smith. London: Tavistock.

Foucault, M. 1975. *Surveiller et punir*. Paris: Gallimard.

(1977a. *Discipline and Punish*, trans. A. Sheridan. New York: Tavistock and London: Allen Lane. New edition 1979, New York: Vintage).

Foucault, M. 1977b. "A Preface to Trangression", trans. D. F. Bouchard and S. Simon, in D. F. Bouchard, ed., *Language, Counter-Memory, Practice*. Ithaca: Cornell University Press.

Foucault, M. 1977c. "Nietzsche, Genealogy, History", trans. D. F. Bouchard and S. Simon, in D.F. Bouchard, ed., *Language, Counter-Memory, Practice*. Ithaca: Cornell University Press.

Foucault, M. 1978. *The History of Sexuality, vol. I: An Introduction*, trans. R. Hurley. New York: Pantheon.

Foucault, M. 1983. "Structuralism and Post-Structuralism: An interview with Michel Foucault", G. Raulet, *Telos* 55.

Foucault, M. 1984. "Nietzsche, Genealogy, and History", in Paul Rabinow, ed., *The Foucault Reader*. New York: Pantheon.

Foucault, M. 1985. *The History of Sexuality, vol. 2, The Use of Pleasure*, trans. R. Hurley. New York: Pantheon.

Foucault, M. 1986. *The History of Sexuality, vol. 3, The Care of the Self*, trans. R. Hurley. New York: Pantheon.

Foucault, M. 1988a. "Technologies of the Self", in Martin, Gutman and Hutton 1988.

Foucault, M. 1988b. "The Political Technology of Individuals", in Martin, Gutman and Hutton 1988.

Foucault, M. 1988c. *Politics, Philosophy, Culture: Interviews and Other Writings, 1977-1984*. New York: Routledge.

Foucault, M. 1991. "Governmentality", trans. R. Braidotti, revised C. Gordon, in Burchell, Gordon and Miller 1991.

Foucault, M. 1993. "Kant on Enlightenment and revolution", trans. C. Gordon, in Gane and Johnson 1993a.

Foucault, M. 1994. *Dits et écrits: 1954-1988*, vol.2. Paris: Gallimard.

Fustel de Coulanges, N. D. 1927. *The Origin of Property in Land*, trans. M. Ashley. London: George Allen and Unwin.

Fustel de Coulanges, N. D. 1956. *The Ancient City: a Study on the Religion, Laws and Institutions of Greece and Rome*, trans. W. Small. New York: Doubleday Anchor Books.

Gane, M. 1988. *On Durkheim's Rules of Sociological Method*. London: Routledge.

Gane, M. 1992. "Introduction: Emile Durkheim, Marcel Mauss and the Sociological Project", in M. Gane, ed., *The Radical Sociology of Durkheim and Mauss*. London: Routledge.

Gane, M. and T. Johnson, eds. 1993a. *Foucault's New Domains*. London: Routledge.

Gane, M. and T. Johnson. 1993b. "Introduction: the Project of Michel Foucault", in Gane and Johnson 1993a.

Garland, D. 1990. *Punishment and Modern Society: A Study in Social Theory*. Oxford: Clarendon Press.

Gatrell, V. A. C., B. Lenman and G. Parker. 1980. *Crime and the Law: The Social History of Crime in Western Europe since 1500*. London: Europa.

Geertz, C. 1983. "Centers, Kings and Charisma: Reflections on the Symbolics of Power" in C. Geertz, *Local Knowledge*. New York: Basic Books.

Geiger, R. 1983. "Durkheimian Sociology under attack: the controversy over sociology in the Ecole Normale Primaires", in Besnard 1983a.

Gephart, W. 1990. *Strafe und Verbrechen: die Theorie Emile Durkheims*. Opladen: Leske & Budrich.

Giddens, A. 1978. *Durkheim: His Life, Work, Writings and Ideas*. Hassocks, Sussex: The Harvester Press.

Gordon, C. 1993. "Question, ethos, event: Foucault on Kant and Enlightenment", in Gane and Johnson 1993a.

Gutting, G. 1989. *Michel Foucault's Archaeology of Scientific Reason*. Cambridge: CUP.

Hacking, I. 1991. "How Should We Do the History of Statistics?", in Burchell, Gordon and Miller 1991.

Halbwachs, M. 1977. "Introduction to the French Edition of 1938", trans. P. Collins, in Durkheim [1938a] 1977a.

Hoskin, K. 1990. "Foucault under examination: the crypto-educationalist unmasked", in Ball 1990a.

Hunt, L. 1988. "The Sacred and the French Revolution", in Alexander 1988a.

Jones, D. 1990. "The genealogy of the urban schoolteacher", in Ball 1990a.

Jones, R. 1990. "Educational practices and scientific knowledge: a genealogical reinterpretation of the emergence of physiology in post-Revolutionary France", in Ball 1990a.

Jones, R. A. and D. A. Kibbee. 1993. "Ambivalent Cartesians: Durkheim, Montesquieu and Method", *American Journal of Sociology*, 100 (1): 1-39.

Karady, V. 1981. "The Prehistory of Present-day French Sociology (1917-57)", in C. C. Lemert, ed., *French Sociology: Rupture and Renewal Since 1968*. New York: Columbia University Press.

Karady, V. 1983. "The Durkheimians in Academe: a reconsideration", in Besnard 1983a.

Lukes, S. 1973. *Emile Durkheim, His Life and Work: A Historical and Critical Study*. London: Allen Lane. (New edition 1992, London: Penguin.)

Lukes, S. and A. Scull. 1984. "Introduction", in S. Lukes and A. Scull, eds., *Durkheim and the Law*. Oxford: Blackwell.

Malinowski, B. 1926. *Crime and Custom in Savage Society*. London: Heinemann.

Marshall, J. D. 1990. "Foucault and educational research", in Ball 1990a.

Martin, L. H., H. Gutman and P. H. Hutton, eds. 1988. *Technologies of the Self: a seminar with Michel Foucault*. Amherst, Massachusetts: University of Massachusetts Press.

Martin, R. 1988. "Truth, Power, Self: an interview with Michel Foucault", in Martin, Gutman and Hutton 1988.

Mauss, M. [1896] 1969. "La religion et les origines du droit pénal d'après un livre récent", in M. Mauss, *Œuvres*, vol. 2, edited by V. Karady. Paris: Editions de Minuit.

Mauss, M. 1925. "Essai sur le don", *Année sociologique*, n.s. 2: 95-176 (1967. *The Gift*, trans. I. Cunnison. London: Routledge & Kegan Paul) (1990. *The Gift*, trans. W. D. Halls. New York: Norton).

Mauss, M. 1985. "A category of the human mind: the notion of person; the notion of self", trans. W. D. Halls, in M. Carruthers, S. Collins and S. Lukes, eds., *The Category of the Person: Anthropology, Philosophy, History*. Cambridge: CUP.

Mead, G. H. 1918. "The Psychology of Punitive Justice", *American Journal of Sociology* 23: 577-602.

Meštrovic S. J. 1988. *Emile Durkheim and the Reformation of Sociology*. Totowa, N. J.: Rowman and Littlefield.

Miller, P. and N. Rose. 1993. "Governing Economic Life", in Gane and Johnson 1993a.

Newell, P., ed. 1972. *A Last Resort? Corporate Punishment in Schools*. Harmondsworth: Penguin.

O'Neill, J. 1986. "The Disciplinary Society: from Weber to Foucault", *British Journal of Sociology* 37: 42-60.

Pasquino, P. 1991. "Theatrum politicum: The genealogy of capital — police and the state of prosperity", in Burchell, Gordon and Miller 1991.

Pasquino, P. 1993. "Michel Foucault (1926-84): The Will to Knowledge", in Gane and Johnson 1993a.

Patton, P. 1979. "Of Power and Prisons", in M. Morris and P. Patton, eds., *Michel Foucault: Power, Truth, Strategy*. Sydney: Feral Press.

Pearce, F. 1989. *The Radical Durkheim*. London: Unwin Hyman.

Pickering, W. S. F. 1990. "The Eternality of the Sacred: Durkheim's Error?", *Archives de sciences sociales des religions*, 69: 91-106.

Procacci, G. 1991. "Social economy and the government of poverty", in Burchell, Gordon and Miller 1991.

Richman, M. 1982. *Reading Georges Bataille: Beyond the Gift*. Baltimore, Maryland: Johns Hopkins University Press.

Richman, M. 1995. "The Sacred Group: A Durkheimian perspective on the Collège de sociologie", in C. B. Gill, ed., *Bataille: Writing the Sacred*. London: Routledge.

Sayer, D. 1991. *Capitalism and Modernity*. New York: Routledge.

Schoenfeld, E. and S. G. Meštrovic. 1991. "From the Sacred Collectivity to the Sacred Individual: The Misunderstood Durkheimian Legacy", *Sociological Focus*, 24 (2).

Schwartz, R.D. and J. C. Miller. 1964. "Legal Evolution and Societal Complexity", *American Journal of Sociology* 70, 159-169.

Selznick, P. 1993. *The Moral Commonwealth*. Berkeley: University of California Press.

Shils, E. 1982. *The Constitution of Society*. Chicago: University of Chicago Press.

Smith, A. 1976. *The Theory of Moral Sentiments*. Oxford: OUP.

Spitzer, S. 1975. "Punishment and Social Organisation", *Law and Society Review* 9: 613-637.

Stock-Morton, P. 1988. *Moral Education for a Secular Society: The Development of Morale Laïque in Nineteenth-Century France*. Albany: State University of New York Press.

Taylor, C. 1985. "The Person", in M. Carruthers, S. Collins and S. Lukes, eds., *The Category of the Person: Anthropology, Philosophy, History*. Cambridge: CUP.

Tole, L.-A. 1993. "Durkheim on Religion and Moral Community in Modernity", *Sociological Inquiry*, 63 (1).

Vogt, W. P. 1983. "Obligation and right: the Durkheimians and the sociology of law", in Besnard 1983a.

Weber, M. 1978. *Economy and Society*, G. Roth and C. Wittich, eds., 2 vols., Berkeley: University of California Press.

Wernick, A. 1984. "Structuralism and the Dislocation of the French Rationalist Project", in J. Fekete, ed., *The Structural Allegory:*

Reconstructive Encounters with the New French Thought. Minneapolis: University of Minnesota Press.

Weisz, G. 1983. "The republican ideology and the social sciences; the Durkheimians and the history of social economy at the Sorbonne", in Besnard 1983a.

Wrong, D. 1994. *The Problem of Order.* New York: Free Press.

INDEX

absolutism, 79, 81, 98
Alexander, Jeffrey, 71
Althusser, Louis, 71, 74, 92
Année sociologique, 66, 72, 73
anomie, 6, 14, 28, 94, 95
Archaeology of Knowledge, 74
Ariès, Philippe, 44, 45
Arnold of Rugby, 45
asceticism, 77
atonement theory, 51
authority, 24, 28, 83; and
  children, 83; and criminal
  justice, 32; and discipline, 53;
  and punishment, 31; evolution
  of, 81; moral, 31, 52; respect
  for, 53
Bachelard, Gaston, 71, 74
Barings, 35
Bataille, Georges, 71, 94, 95
Bentham, Jeremy, 87
biopolitics, 88
biopower, 92
body, 10
Bourgeois, Léon, 88
Brecht, Bertolt, 98
Brochier, J. J., 68
Brunschvicg, Léon, 6
Caillois, Roger, 94
cane, the, 55
Canguilhem, Georges, 71, 74
Care of the Self, 84
categories, 95–97
child psychology, 53
children, 82; as conscious
  citizens, 83; Jewish, 43
Christian doctrines, 44

Christianity, 85
citizenship, 79, 81, 82, 94
classifications, 95
classroom, 23, 24, 50, 83
collective emotion, 21
collective representations,
  11, 76
Collège de France, 10
Collège de Sociologie, 94
communal welfare, 89
communitarianism, 94
community service orders,
  34
Comte, Auguste, 73–75, 90,
  95
conscience, 82; moral, 44
conscience collective, 19,
  20, 22, 23, 26, 28, 64, 65;
  and crime, 65
contracts, 19, 97
copying, as punishment, 46
corporal punishment, 83;
  abolition of, 45, 56; and
  humanism, 42; and parents
  rights, 56; and Third
  Republic, 42; as training,
  40; French public opinion,
  45; in Britain, 45, 55; in
  France, 45; in schools, 41;
  in the past, 43; Jewish, 43,
  55; morality of, 40;
  rejection by Durkheim, 41,
  42; today, 54
Cours de science sociale, 60,
  61
Craig, J. E., 72

115

119